Cuisinart Convection Toaster Oven Airfryer Cookbook

1001-Day Mouth-Watering, Budget-Friendly Cuisinart Recipes to Bake, Broil, Toast, Convection and More

Srein Heban

© Copyright 2021 Srein Heban - All Rights Reserved.

In no way is it legal to reproduce, duplicate, or transmit any part of this document by either electronic means or in printed format. Recording of this publication is strictly prohibited, and any storage of this material is not allowed unless with written permission from the publisher. All rights reserved.

The information provided herein is stated to be truthful and consistent, in that any liability, regarding inattention or otherwise, by any usage or abuse of any policies, processes, or directions contained within is the solitary and complete responsibility of the recipient reader. Under no circumstances will any legal liability or blame be held against the publisher for any reparation, damages, or monetary loss due to the information herein, either directly or indirectly.

Respective authors own all copyrights not held by the publisher.

Legal Notice:

This book is copyright protected. This is only for personal use. You cannot amend, distribute, sell, use, quote or paraphrase any part of the content within this book without the consent of the author or copyright owner. Legal action will be pursued if this is breached.

Disclaimer Notice:

Please note the information contained within this document is for educational and entertainment purposes only. Every attempt has been made to provide accurate, up-to-date and reliable, complete information. No warranties of any kind are expressed or implied. Readers acknowledge that the author is not engaging in the rendering of legal, financial, medical or professional advice.

By reading this document, the reader agrees that under no circumstances are we responsible for any losses, direct or indirect, which are incurred as a result of the use of information contained within this document, including, but not limited to, errors, omissions, or inaccuracies.

Table of Contents

- Introduction 5
- **Chapter 1: Cuisinart Convection Toaster Oven Airfryer Basics** 5
  - What is Cuisinart Convection Toaster Oven Airfryer? 6
  - Features of Cuisinart Art Air Fryer Toaster Oven 6
  - Cooking Functions 8
  - Benefits of Using Cuisinart Convection Toaster Oven Airfryer 9
  - Tips 11
- **Chapter 2: Breakfast & Brunch** 12
  - Breakfast Oatmeal Cake 12
  - Healthy Baked Oatmeal 13
  - Easy Cheese Egg Casserole 14
  - Spicy Egg Casserole 15
  - Delicious Baked Eggs 16
  - Healthy Bran Muffins 17
  - Spinach Zucchini Egg Muffins 18
  - Quick & Easy Granola 19
  - Flavorful Pumpkin Bread 20
  - Ham Egg Muffins 21
  - Easy Breakfast Bake 22
  - Easy Egg Quiche 23
  - Moist Orange Bread Loaf 24
  - Cinnamon Sweet Potatoes 25
  - Baked Breakfast Quiche 26
- **Chapter 3: Poultry** 27
  - Baked Chicken Fritters 27
  - Juicy Baked Chicken Breast 28
  - Chicken Burger Patties 29
  - Green Chili Chicken Noodle Casserole 30
  - Potato Garlic Chicken 31
  - Baked Spinach Cheese Chicken 32
  - Honey Chicken Wings 33
  - Baked Zucchini Chicken Tenders .. 34
  - Simple Jerk Chicken Wings 35
  - Cracker Apple Chicken 36
  - Meatballs 37
  - Sweet & Spicy Chicken Wings 38
  - Air Fryer Chicken Tenders 39
  - Easy BBQ Chicken Drumsticks 40
  - Greek Chicken Breast 41
- **Chapter 4: Beef, Pork & Lamb** 42
  - Stuffed Pork Chops 42
  - Spicy Meatballs 43
  - Perfect Beef Hash brown Bake 44
  - Curried Beef Patties 45
  - Flavorful Sirloin Steak 46
  - Meatballs 47
  - Delicious Pork Belly 48
  - Ranch Pork Chops 49
  - Meatballs 50
  - Baked Pork Tenderloin 51
  - Tasty Steak Tips 52
  - Spiced Pork Chops 53
  - Ranch Beef Patties 54
  - Delicious Air Fryer Kebabs 55
  - Honey Garlic Pork Chops 56
- **Chapter 5: Fish & Seafood** 57
  - Spicy Halibut 57
  - Basil Tomato Salmon 58
  - Easy Blackened Shrimp 59
  - Lemon Butter Shrimp 60
  - Tender & Juicy Cajun Cod 61
  - Spicy Baked Shrimp 62
  - Spicy Catfish 63
  - Greek Cod with Asparagus 64
  - Perfect Crab Cakes 65
  - Dijon Salmon Fillets 66
  - Air Fry Prawns 67
  - Miso White Fish Fillets 68
  - Rosemary Garlic Shrimp 69
  - Italian Cod 70
  - Air Fry Tuna Patties 71
- **Chapter 6: Vegetables & Side Dishes** 72
  - Baked Vegetables 72
  - Baked Cauliflower & Tomatoes 73
  - Baked Apple Sweet Potatoes 74
  - Jalapeno Bread 75

Tasty Butternut Squash 76	Chili Lime Sweet Potatoes 82
Air Fried Eggplant Cubes 77	Broccoli Olives Tomatoes 83
Cheese Herb Zucchini 78	Tasty Hassel Back Potatoes 84
Parmesan Baked Asparagus 79	Cheesy Squash Casserole 85
Ranch Potatoes 80	Air-Fried Herb Mushrooms 86
Baked Ratatouille 81	

Chapter 7: Snacks & Appetizers 87

Cheesy Spinach Dip........................ 87	Healthy Baked Pecans 95
Air Fryer Mixed Nuts 88	Coconut Broccoli Pop-Corn 96
Flavorful Crab Dip.......................... 89	Cheese Garlic Dip............................ 97
Jalapeno Spinach Dip 90	Shrimp Kebabs 98
Vegetables Balls.............................. 91	Air Fryer Nuts 99
Zucchini Coconut Bites 92	Air Fryer Paprika Almonds 100
Air Fryer Radish Chips 93	Cheddar Dill Mushrooms............... 101
Crispy Eggplant Bites 94	

Chapter 8: Desserts 102

Strawberry Cobbler 102	Tasty Gingersnap Cookies 110
Delicious Raspberry Cobbler......... 103	Flavorful Coconut Cake 111
Vanilla Butter Cake 104	Orange Almond Muffins 112
Easy Blueberry Muffins 105	Almond Blueberry Bars................. 113
Vanilla Banana Brownies............... 106	Strawberry Muffins........................ 114
Mini Brownie Muffins 107	Easy Ricotta Cake........................... 115
Cream Cheese Butter Cake 108	Tasty Pumpkin Cookies 116
Vanilla Lemon Cupcakes............... 109	

Conclusion 117

Introduction

Are you tired of cooking the same dishes over and over again? Don't you have any new recipes to make and give to your family and friends? Are you tired of always having to buy new products that are rarely used and likely to be thrown away? Cuisinart Convection Toaster Oven Air fryer will provide you with a multifunctional appliance in the kitchen to prepare various dishes, even at the same time, and ensure healthy cooking with a reduced fat content, perfect for any nutritional need.

With Cuisinart Convection Toaster Oven Air fryer Cookbook, you can set programs to cook French fries, fish, chicken, toasts. Still, you will also find all the advice and recipes to cook many other dishes, with the correct cooking times and recommended temperature, always to get the best possible result.

Chapter 1: Cuisinart Convection Toaster Oven Airfryer Basics

What is Cuisinart Convection Toaster Oven Airfryer?

The Cuisinart Convection Toaster Oven Airfryer is an innovative and advanced cooking appliance used to perform different cooking techniques. As its name indicates that, it works as an oven toaster and air fryer these three different cooking techniques make it a unique cooking appliance.

The Cuisinart Convection Toaster Oven Airfryer is working on 1800 watt and it is made up of a sturdy stainless steel body that gives sleek look to your Cuisinart oven. It is one of the multifunctional cooking appliances not only Air fry your food but also performs different operations like broil, toast, bake and warm, etc. Due to large capacity, you can toast 6 bread slices at a time, roast 4 pounds of chicken, and bake a 12-inch pizza.

It allows you to cook lots of different dishes like meat, poultry, fish, desserts, vegetables, and fruits. It runs on hot air circulation techniques in which hot air is circulating into the cooking chamber with the help of a convection fan situated at the top side of the oven. Using this technique Cuisinart Convection Toaster Oven Airfryer cooks your food faster and evenly from all the sides. It fries your favourite French fries, chicken wings, and shrimp with very little oil or no oil. It is one of the healthier ways to prepare your favourite food faster.

Features of Cuisinart Art Air Fryer Toaster Oven

The Cuisinart Convection Toaster Oven Airfryer is loaded with various features that make your daily cooking easiest, fastest, and safest way. These features are:

- **Power LED indicator**

The power light is illuminated continuously when the oven is in use. Continuous light illuminates indicates that when the oven is in use the exterior wall of the oven gets very hot.

- **On/Oven Timer Dial**

The timer dial is used to set the desire cooking time as per your recipe needs. The timer range is set in between 1 minute to 1 hour. When the timer is finished the oven is turned off. You cannot use the timer dial while using the toast function.

- **Temperature Dial**

The temperature dial helps you to set the desire temperature setting as per your recipe needs. The dial temperature range starts in between 150°F to 450°F.

- **Function Dial**

The function dial is used to select desire cooking functions from warm, broil, toast, bake, and air fry.

- **On/ Toast Timer dial**

This function allows you to select the desire toast shade from light, medium to dark. First set the function dialer at toast position then select the desired shade from the toasting dial. When the desire cooking cycle is completed the oven is power off automatically.

- **Light Button**

Using this button you can switch on the oven interior light to see the cooking process when the oven door is closed.

- **Pull Crumb Tray**

The Crumb tray is situated at the front bottom side of the oven. You can pull it out to easily clean for crumbs, bits, and pieces of foods fallen during baking or grilling

- **Air Fryer Basket**

It is recommended that while using the air fryer function you can use the air fryer basket seated into baking pan/drip tray to avoid the mess created during the air frying process.

- **Baking Pan/ Drip Tray**

As per your convenience, you can use it while you are roasting or baking your food. You can also use it while air frying your food to prevent spills residues.

- **Safety Auto OFF Door Switch**

The Cuisinart Convection Toaster Oven Airfryer is equipped with a safety auto-off door switch which automatically shuts off the oven power supply if the oven door is opened.

- **Cord Storage**

At the backside of the oven, cord storage is given to store excess cord to keep your kitchen countertop clean and neat.

Cooking Functions

The Cuisinart Convection Toaster Oven Airfryer comes with 5 different cooking functions these functions include:

1. **Warm**

This function is used to keep your food warm until it to be served. You can also reheat your leftover food or frozen food using this function. It keeps your food warm and makes your air fried food crisp again.

To use this function set your oven rack at rack 2 position. Then set the temperature dial at the warm position and function dial at warm. Select the desired time for warming your food using a timer dial. While the warming cycle is going on the power led illuminates and when the warming cycle has been completed the oven is automatically power off itself.

2. **Broil Convection Broil**

This function is used to broil your favourite burgers, melting cheese, and toppings spread over sandwiches. The combination of broil and convection gives a nice brown texture to your favourite meat and fish from all the sides.

While using this function first place the air fryer rack over a baking pan and set it into the rack to the position. Then set the function dial at broil convection position and temperature dial position to Toast/Broil position. Select the desire cooking time to start the actual broiling process. After finishing the cooking cycle the oven is automatically power off itself.

3. **Toast**

Using this function you can toast your favourite sandwich, bread, and warmed up your waffle.

To toast food first place your food in centre position at oven rack or baking pan and set it at rack position 2 for toasting purpose. Then set the function dial at toast position and temperature dial at Toast/Broil position. Turn the toast timer dial and select the desired shade from light, med, and dark. When the toasting cycle is complete the timer will ring and the oven automatically powers off.

4. **Bake Convection Bake**

This setting is ideal for baking your favourite foods. Using this setting you can bake casseroles, cakes, pastry, muffins, and cookies. With the help of convection fan hot air is blows fast into the cooking chamber and it gives you baking as well as browning results. You can make roast meat and make 8*11 inch pizza into baking pan.

To start baking first set the function dial at the bake convection bake position and select the desire temperature level with the help of the temperature dial. Turn and select the appropriate cooking time as per recipe needs. After finishing the baking cycle oven power off automatically. To get the best baking results always preheat your oven for 5 minutes prior.

5. **Air Fry**

This function is used to air fry your favourite foods like French fries, onion rings, chicken wings, and more. This is one of the healthy methods of frying your favourite food quickly and easily. It gives a nice crispy and crunchy texture to your food.

To air fry, your food first places the air fry rack into baking try and set it into rack position 2. Then set the function dial at air fry position and select desire temperature settings. Turn the timer dial and select the desired time as per recipe needs. When the cooking cycle is complete the oven is automatically powered off.

Benefits of Using Cuisinart Convection Toaster Oven Airfryer

The Cuisinart Toaster oven is one of the multi-functional cooking appliances that work as an air fryer, oven, and toaster come with various benefits.

- **Cooks healthy Food**

Compare to the deep-frying method Cuisinart Convection Toaster Oven Airfryer requires very little oil to cook your food. You cook a wide variety of fried food like French fries, chicken wings, onion rings within a tablespoon of oil without compromising the taste and texture of food. It encourages you to change your daily eating habits towards healthy eating. Air fried food is one of the healthiest choices for daily cooking. They are lower in calories, fats, and some harmful compounds found in the traditional deep frying method.

- **Versatile Cooking Appliance**

The Cuisinart oven is performing operations of air fryer, oven, and toaster. You can use it for different operations like Air fry your French fries, broil meat or fish, toast bread or sandwich, bake your favourite cake and also keep your food warm. All these operations are made into a single appliance; you never need to buy a separate cooking appliance for each operation. It not only saves your time and energy but also saves your money.

- **Cooks your food faster**

The Cuisinart oven is loaded with a hot air circulation mechanism situated at the top side of the oven. It blows the hottest air with the help of a convection fan and cooks your food fast and evenly from all the sides. The oven consumes 1800 watt power to blow 450°F hot air which cooks your food quickly as compared to the traditional cooking method.

- **Cooks large quantity of food**

The Cuisinart oven is specially designed to hold more food. It comes with 2 rack positions and holds a large quantity of food at a time. The small frame and large interior allows you to bake a 12-inch pizza or air fry 3 pounds of chicken wings and also make a 12-inch pizza. Due to small and compact design, it also saves your kitchen countertop space.

- **Easy to clean**

The interior of the Cuisinart oven is coated with non-stick coating makes the daily cleaning process easy. The oven comes with a user manual you just need to follow the cleaning instructions as per given in the manual.

Tips

1. **Air Frying Tips**
   - Different types of oils are used while air frying your food. If you want mild flavour then use canola, vegetable, and grape-seed oil. If you want rich flavour then use olive oil during air fry.
   - Always flip the large food items like chicken cutlets during halfway of the cooking process. This will ensure that the food is cooked evenly from all the sides with a brown texture.
   - Do not crowd the food while air frying; this will affect the even cooking result, taste, and texture of food.
   - Cut food into even sizes, this will help to cook food more evenly and quickly.

2. **Broiling Tips**
   - To get a perfect broiling result always put the air fryer rack into the baking tray during the broiling process.
   - Use a sturdy metal pan during broiling. Do not use any glass while broiling even if the glass is strong.
   - To get a perfect broiling result to arrange food items in a single layer. This will ensure even cooking and browning results.

3. **Baking Tips**
   - A larger food item like chicken is placed into rack 1 position and while baking pizza use baking pan at rack 1 position.
   - Before start, the baking process always preheats your oven to get quick and perfect baking results.

4. **Toasting Tips**
   - Place your bread at the centre position of the oven to get even toasting results.
   - Always keep watch on your food from the oven window while toasting your food until how the oven cooks your food while toasting.

Chapter 2: Breakfast & Brunch

Breakfast Oatmeal Cake

Preparation Time: 10 minutes
Cooking Time: 25 minutes
Serve: 8

Ingredients:

- 2 eggs
- 1 tbsp coconut oil
- 3 tbsp yogurt
- 1/2 tsp baking powder
- 1 tsp cinnamon
- 1 tsp vanilla
- 3 tbsp honey
- 1/2 tsp baking soda
- 1 apple, peel & chopped
- 1 cup oats

Directions:

1. Fit the Cuisinart oven with the rack in position 1.
2. Line baking dish with parchment paper and set aside.
3. Add 3/4 cup oats and remaining ingredients into the blender and blend until smooth.
4. Add remaining oats and stir well.
5. Pour mixture into the prepared baking dish.
6. Set to bake at 350 F for 30 minutes. After 5 minutes place the baking dish in the preheated oven.
7. Slice and serve.

Nutritional Value (Amount per Serving):

- Calories 114
- Fat 3.6 g
- Carbohydrates 18.2 g
- Sugar 10 g
- Protein 3.2 g
- Cholesterol 41 mg

Healthy Baked Oatmeal

Preparation Time: 10 minutes

Cooking Time: 20 minutes

Serve: 6

Ingredients:

- 1 egg
- 1/3 cup dried cranberries
- 1 tsp vanilla
- 1 1/2 tsp cinnamon
- 2 tbsp butter, melted
- 1/2 cup applesauce
- 1 1/2 cups milk
- 1 tsp baking powder
- 1/3 cup light brown sugar
- 2 cups old fashioned oats
- 1/4 tsp salt

Directions:

1. Fit the Cuisinart oven with the rack in position 1.
2. Grease 8*8-inch baking dish and set aside.
3. In a bowl, mix egg, vanilla, butter, applesauce, baking powder, cinnamon, brown sugar, oats, and salt.
4. Add milk and stir well.
5. Add cranberries and fold well.
6. Pour mixture into the prepared baking dish.
7. Set to bake at 350 F for 25 minutes. After 5 minutes place the baking dish in the preheated oven.
8. Serve and enjoy.

Nutritional Value (Amount per Serving):

- Calories 330
- Fat 9.3 g
- Carbohydrates 50.6 g
- Sugar 14.4 g
- Protein 9.7 g
- Cholesterol 42 mg

Easy Cheese Egg Casserole

Preparation Time: 10 minutes

Cooking Time: 40 minutes

Serve: 10

Ingredients:

- 12 eggs
- 8 oz cheddar cheese, shredded
- 1/3 cup milk
- 1/4 tsp pepper
- 1 tsp salt

Directions:

1. Fit the Cuisinart oven with the rack in position 1.
2. Spray 9*13-inch casserole dish with cooking spray and set aside.
3. In a bowl, whisk eggs with milk, pepper, and salt.
4. Add shredded cheese and stir well.
5. Pour egg mixture into the prepared casserole dish.
6. Set to bake at 350 F for 45 minutes. After 5 minutes place the casserole dish in the preheated oven.
7. Serve and enjoy.

Nutritional Value (Amount per Serving):

- Calories 171
- Fat 12.9 g
- Carbohydrates 1.1 g
- Sugar 0.9 g
- Protein 12.6 g
- Cholesterol 221 mg

Spicy Egg Casserole

Preparation Time: 10 minutes

Cooking Time: 45 minutes

Serve: 8

Ingredients:

- 10 eggs
- 1 cup Colby jack cheese, shredded
- 1 cup cottage cheese
- 1 tsp baking powder
- 1/3 cup flour
- 1/2 cup milk
- 4.5 oz can green chilies, chopped
- 1/2 small onion, minced
- 2 tbsp butter
- 1 tsp seasoned salt

Directions:

1. Fit the Cuisinart oven with the rack in position 1.
2. Spray 9*13-inch casserole dish with cooking spray and set aside.
3. Melt butter in a pan over medium heat.
4. Add onion and green chilies and sauté for 5 minutes. Remove pan from heat and set aside.
5. In a small bowl, whisk milk, baking powder, and flour until smooth.
6. In a mixing bowl, whisk eggs with cheese, cottage cheese, and seasoned salt.
7. Add sautéed onion and green chilies, milk, and flour mixture to the eggs and whisk until well combined.
8. Pour egg mixture into the prepared casserole dish.
9. Set to bake at 350 F for 50 minutes. After 5 minutes place the casserole dish in the preheated oven.
10. Serve and enjoy.

Nutritional Value (Amount per Serving):

- Calories 219
- Fat 13.8 g
- Carbohydrates 8.4 g
- Sugar 1.4 g
- Protein 14.9 g
- Cholesterol 228 mg

Delicious Baked Eggs

Preparation Time: 10 minutes

Cooking Time: 45 minutes

Serve: 8

Ingredients:

- 12 eggs
- 1/2 cup all-purpose flour
- 16 oz cottage cheese
- 16 oz cheddar cheese, shredded
- 1 tsp salt

Directions:

1. Fit the Cuisinart oven with the rack in position 1.
2. Grease 9*13-inch baking pan with butter and set aside.
3. In a large bowl, whisk eggs with flour, cottage cheese, cheddar cheese, and salt.
4. Pour egg mixture into the prepared baking pan.
5. Set to bake at 350 F for 50 minutes. After 5 minutes place the baking pan in the preheated oven.
6. Serve and enjoy.

Nutritional Value (Amount per Serving):

- Calories 402
- Fat 26.5 g
- Carbohydrates 9.3 g
- Sugar 1 g
- Protein 31 g
- Cholesterol 310 mg

Healthy Bran Muffins

Preparation Time: 10 minutes

Cooking Time: 20 minutes

Serve: 12

Ingredients:

- 2 eggs
- 1 cup milk
- 1 1/2 cups wheat bran
- 1/4 cup molasses
- 1/4 cup white sugar
- 1/4 cup brown sugar
- 1/4 cup shortening
- 1/2 cup raisins
- 1/4 tsp cinnamon
- 1/2 tsp baking soda
- 1 1/2 tsp baking powder
- 1 cup flour
- 1/2 tsp salt

Directions:

1. Fit the Cuisinart oven with the rack in position 1.
2. Line a 12-cup muffin tray with cupcake liners and set aside.
3. In a bowl, mix flour, raisins, cinnamon, baking soda, baking powder, flour, and salt.
4. In a separate bowl, beat sugar and shortening using a hand mixer until fluffy.
5. Add eggs and molasses and beat until well combined. Add bran and milk and stir well.
6. Add flour mixture and mix until just combined.
7. Pour mixture into the prepared muffin tray.
8. Set to bake at 400 F for 25 minutes. After 5 minutes place the muffin tray in the preheated oven.
9. Serve and enjoy.

Nutritional Value (Amount per Serving):

- Calories 178
- Fat 5.9 g
- Carbohydrates 31 g
- Sugar 15.5 g
- Protein 4 g
- Cholesterol 29 mg

Spinach Zucchini Egg Muffins

Preparation Time: 10 minutes

Cooking Time: 20 minutes

Serve: 12

Ingredients:

- 8 eggs
- 1 cup baby spinach, chopped
- 1 red bell pepper, diced
- 1/4 cup green onion, chopped
- 12 bacon slices, cooked and crumbled
- 2 small zucchini, sliced
- 1/4 cup almond milk
- 2 tbsp parsley, chopped
- 1 tbsp olive oil
- Pepper
- Salt

Directions:

1. Fit the Cuisinart oven with the rack in position 1.
2. Spray 12-cups muffin tin with cooking spray and set aside.
3. Heat olive oil in a pan over medium heat.
4. Add parsley, spinach, green onion, red bell pepper to the pan and sauté until spinach is wilted.
5. In a bowl, whisk eggs with almond milk, pepper, and salt.
6. Add sautéed vegetables, bacon, and zucchini to the egg mixture and stir well.
7. Pour egg mixture into the greased muffin tin.
8. Set to bake at 350 F for 25 minutes, after 5 minutes, place muffin tin in the oven.
9. Serve and enjoy.

Nutritional Value (Amount per Serving):

- Calories 174
- Fat 13.3 g
- Carbohydrates 2.5 g
- Sugar 1.3 g
- Protein 11.3 g
- Cholesterol 130 mg

Quick & Easy Granola

Preparation Time: 10 minutes

Cooking Time: 8 minutes

Serve: 4

Ingredients:

- 2 cups oats
- 2 tbsp chia seeds
- 1 tsp vanilla
- 1/2 tsp cinnamon
- 1/4 cup honey
- 1/4 cup almond butter

Directions:

1. Fit the Cuisinart oven with the rack in position 1.
2. In a bowl, mix the almond butter, honey, cinnamon, and vanilla.
3. Add oats and chia seeds and mix well.
4. Transfer oats mixture onto the parchment-lined baking pan.
5. Place the baking pan in Cuisinart oven and set to bake at 350 F for 8 minutes.
6. Serve and enjoy.

Nutritional Value (Amount per Serving):

- Calories 248
- Fat 4.4 g
- Carbohydrates 47.3 g
- Sugar 18 g
- Protein 6.3 g
- Cholesterol 6.3 mg

Flavorful Pumpkin Bread

Preparation Time: 10 minutes

Cooking Time: 55 minutes

Serve: 12

Ingredients:

- 2 eggs
- 8 oz pumpkin puree
- 1 3/4 cups flour
- 1 1/2 cups sugar
- 1/3 cup water
- 1/2 cup vegetable oil
- 1/8 tsp ground ginger
- 1/4 tsp ground cloves
- 1/2 tsp ground nutmeg
- 1/2 tsp ground cinnamon
- 1 tsp baking soda
- 3/4 tsp salt

Directions:

1. Fit the Cuisinart oven with the rack in position 1.
2. In a bowl, whisk eggs, sugar, water, oil, and pumpkin puree until combined.
3. In a separate bowl, mix dry ingredients.
4. Add dry ingredient mixture into the egg mixture and mix until well combined.
5. Pour batter into the greased loaf pan.
6. Set to bake at 350 F for 60 minutes, after 5 minutes, place the loaf pan in the oven.
7. Slice and serve.

Nutritional Value (Amount per Serving):

- Calories 258
- Fat 10.1 g
- Carbohydrates 40.7 g
- Sugar 25.8 g
- Protein 3 g
- Cholesterol 27 mg

Ham Egg Muffins

Preparation Time: 10 minutes

Cooking Time: 20 minutes

Serve: 12

Ingredients:

- 12 eggs
- 2 cups ham, diced
- 1 3/4 cup cheddar cheese, shredded
- 1/2 pepper
- 1/2 tsp salt

Directions:

1. Fit the Cuisinart oven with the rack in position 1.
2. Spray 12-cups muffin tin with cooking spray and set aside.
3. In a bowl, whisk eggs with pepper and salt.
4. Stir in cheddar cheese and ham.
5. Pour egg mixture into prepared muffin tin.
6. Set to bake at 375 F for 25 minutes, after 5 minutes, place the muffin tin in the oven.
7. Serve and enjoy.

Nutritional Value (Amount per Serving):

- Calories 166
- Fat 11.8 g
- Carbohydrates 1.5 g
- Sugar 0.4 g
- Protein 13.4 g
- Cholesterol 194 mg

Easy Breakfast Bake

Preparation Time: 10 minutes

Cooking Time: 45 minutes

Serve: 6

Ingredients:

- 10 eggs
- 10 bacon sliced, cooked, and crumbled
- 2 tomatoes, sliced
- 1 tbsp butter
- 3 cups baby spinach, chopped
- 1/2 tsp salt

Directions:

1. Fit the Cuisinart oven with the rack in position 1.
2. Melt butter in a pan.
3. Add spinach and cook until spinach wilted.
4. Whisk eggs and salt in a bowl. Add spinach and whisk well.
5. Pour egg mixture into the greased 9-inch baking dish. Top with bacon and tomatoes
6. Set to bake at 350 F for 50 minutes, after 5 minutes, place the baking dish in the oven.
7. Serve and enjoy.

Nutritional Value (Amount per Serving):

- Calories 266
- Fat 21 g
- Carbohydrates 2.7 g
- Sugar 1.7 g
- Protein 18.4 g
- Cholesterol 303 mg

Easy Egg Quiche

Preparation Time: 10 minutes

Cooking Time: 45 minutes

Serve: 6

Ingredients:

- 8 eggs
- 4 tbsp butter, melted
- 6 oz cream cheese
- 6 oz cheddar cheese, shredded

Directions:

1. Fit the Cuisinart oven with the rack in position 1.
2. Add eggs, cheese, butter, and cream cheese into the bowl and whisk until well combined.
3. Pour egg mixture into the greased pie dish.
4. Set to bake at 325 F for 50 minutes, after 5 minutes, place the pie dish in the oven.
5. Serve and enjoy.

Nutritional Value (Amount per Serving):

- Calories 365
- Fat 32.8 g
- Carbohydrates 1.6 g
- Sugar 0.7 g
- Protein 16.7 g
- Cholesterol 300 mg

Moist Orange Bread Loaf

Preparation Time: 10 minutes

Cooking Time: 50 minutes

Serve: 10

Ingredients:

- 4 eggs
- 4 oz butter, softened
- 1 cup of orange juice
- 1 orange zest, grated
- 1 cup of sugar
- 2 tsp baking powder
- 2 cups all-purpose flour
- 1 tsp vanilla

Directions:

1. Fit the Cuisinart oven with the rack in position 1.
2. In a large bowl, whisk eggs and sugar until creamy.
3. Whisk in vanilla, butter, orange juice, and orange zest.
4. Add flour and baking powder and mix until combined.
5. Pour batter into the greased 9*5-inch loaf pan.
6. Set to bake at 350 F for 55 minutes, after 5 minutes, place the loaf pan in the oven.
7. Slice and serve.

Nutritional Value (Amount per Serving):

- Calories 286
- Fat 11.3 g
- Carbohydrates 42.5 g
- Sugar 22.4 g
- Protein 5.1 g
- Cholesterol 90 mg

Cinnamon Sweet Potatoes

Preparation Time: 10 minutes

Cooking Time: 45 minutes

Serve: 6

Ingredients:

- 2 lbs sweet potatoes, peel and cut into 1/2-inch cubes
- 1/2 tsp chili powder
- 1/2 tsp cinnamon
- 2 tbsp olive oil
- 1/2 tsp onion powder
- 1/2 tsp garlic powder
- Pepper
- Salt

Directions:

1. Fit the Cuisinart oven with the rack in position 1.
2. Line baking pan with parchment paper and set aside.
3. Spread sweet potato cubes in a prepared baking pan.
4. Drizzle with oil and sprinkle with spices. Toss to coat.
5. Set to bake at 400 F for 50 minutes, after 5 minutes, place the baking pan in the oven.
6. Serve and enjoy.

Nutritional Value (Amount per Serving):

- Calories 221
- Fat 5 g
- Carbohydrates 42.8 g
- Sugar 0.9 g
- Protein 2.4 g
- Cholesterol 0 mg

Baked Breakfast Quiche

Preparation Time: 10 minutes

Cooking Time: 45 minutes

Serve: 6

Ingredients:

- 6 eggs
- 1 cup milk
- 1 cup cheddar cheese, grated
- 1 cup tomatoes, chopped
- Pepper
- Salt

Directions:

1. Fit the Cuisinart oven with the rack in position 1.
2. In a bowl, whisk eggs with cheese, milk, pepper, and salt. Stir in tomatoes.
3. Pour egg mixture into the greased pie dish.
4. Set to bake at 350 F for 50 minutes, after 5 minutes, place the pie dish in the oven.
5. Serve and enjoy.

Nutritional Value (Amount per Serving):

- Calories 165
- Fat 11.5 g
- Carbohydrates 3.8 g
- Sugar 3.1 g
- Protein 11.8 g
- Cholesterol 187 mg

Chapter 3: Poultry

Baked Chicken Fritters

Preparation Time: 10 minutes
Cooking Time: 25 minutes
Serve: 4

Ingredients:

- 1 lb ground chicken
- 1 cup breadcrumbs
- 1 egg, lightly beaten
- 1 garlic clove, minced
- 1 1/2 cup mozzarella cheese, shredded
- 1/2 cup shallots, chopped
- 2 cups broccoli, chopped
- Pepper
- Salt

Directions:

1. Fit the Cuisinart oven with the rack in position 1.
2. Add all ingredients into the bowl and mix until well combined.
3. Make small patties and place them in a parchment-lined baking pan.
4. Set to bake at 390 F for 30 minutes. After 5 minutes place the baking pan in the preheated oven.
5. Serve and enjoy.

Nutritional Value (Amount per Serving):

- Calories 399
- Fat 13 g
- Carbohydrates 26.5 g
- Sugar 2.5 g
- Protein 42.6 g
- Cholesterol 147 mg

Juicy Baked Chicken Breast

Preparation Time: 10 minutes

Cooking Time: 25 minutes

Serve: 4

Ingredients:

- 4 chicken breasts
- 1 tbsp fresh parsley, chopped
- 1/4 tsp red pepper flakes
- 1/2 tsp black pepper
- 1 tsp Italian seasoning
- 2 tbsp olive oil
- 1/4 cup balsamic vinegar
- 1 tsp kosher salt

Directions:

1. Fit the Cuisinart oven with the rack in position 1.
2. Place chicken breasts into the mixing bowl.
3. Mix together remaining ingredients and pour over chicken breasts and coat well and let marinate for 30 minutes.
4. Arrange marinated chicken breasts into a greased baking dish.
5. Set to bake at 425 F for 30 minutes. After 5 minutes place the baking dish in the preheated oven.
6. Slice and serve.

Nutritional Value (Amount per Serving):

- Calories 345
- Fat 18.2 g
- Carbohydrates 0.6 g
- Sugar 0.2 g
- Protein 42.3 g
- Cholesterol 131 mg

Chicken Burger Patties

Preparation Time: 10 minutes

Cooking Time: 25 minutes

Serve: 4

Ingredients:

- 1 lb ground chicken
- 1 egg, lightly beaten
- 1 cup cheddar cheese, shredded
- 1 cup carrot, grated
- 1 cup cauliflower, grated
- 1/8 tsp red pepper flakes
- 2 garlic cloves, minced
- 1/2 cup onion, minced
- 3/4 cup breadcrumbs
- Pepper
- Salt

Directions:

1. Fit the Cuisinart oven with the rack in position 1.
2. Add all ingredients into the bowl and mix until well combined.
3. Make small patties and place them in a parchment-lined baking pan.
4. Set to bake at 400 F for 30 minutes. After 5 minutes place the baking pan in the preheated oven.
5. Serve and enjoy.

Nutritional Value (Amount per Serving):

- Calories 451
- Fat 20 g
- Carbohydrates 20.9 g
- Sugar 4.1 g
- Protein 44.9 g
- Cholesterol 172 mg

Green Chili Chicken Noodle Casserole

Preparation Time: 10 minutes

Cooking Time: 30 minutes

Serve: 6

Ingredients:

- 3 cups cooked chicken, shredded
- 4 oz can green chilies
- 1/3 cup parmesan cheese, shredded
- 3 cups cheddar cheese, shredded
- 1 1/3 cups milk
- 10.5 oz cream of chicken soup
- 1 tsp chili powder
- 1 onion, diced
- 1/3 cup bell pepper, diced
- 3 tbsp butter
- 3 cups shell noodles, uncooked
- 1/2 tsp salt

Directions:

1. Fit the Cuisinart oven with the rack in position 1.
2. Cook noodles according to the packet instructions and drain well.
3. Melt butter in a pan over medium heat.
4. Add bell pepper and onion and sauté for 5 minutes. Stir in chili powder and salt.
5. In a large bowl, mix chicken soup, parmesan cheese, 2 cups cheddar cheese, milk, and sautéed onion bell pepper. Stir in green chilies, noodles, and chicken.
6. Pour mixture into the greased 9*13-inch baking dish and top with remaining cheese.
7. Set to bake at 375 F for 35 minutes. After 5 minutes place the baking dish in the preheated oven.
8. Serve and enjoy.

Nutritional Value (Amount per Serving):

- Calories 560
- Fat 32.6 g
- Carbohydrates 23.9 g
- Sugar 5 g
- Protein 42.2 g
- Cholesterol 156 mg

Potato Garlic Chicken

Preparation Time: 10 minutes
Cooking Time: 25 minutes
Serve: 4

Ingredients:

- 4 chicken breasts, skinless & boneless
- 1/2 cup cheddar cheese, shredded
- 1 cup mozzarella cheese, shredded
- 2 tsp dried parsley
- 1/2 tsp crushed red pepper
- 1 tbsp garlic, minced
- 1/2 cup butter
- 1 lb baby potatoes, cut into half
- 1/4 tsp pepper
- 1/4 tsp salt

Directions:

1. Fit the Cuisinart oven with the rack in position 1.
2. Season chicken with pepper and salt and place in a casserole dish. Top with potatoes.
3. Melt butter in a pan over medium heat. Add garlic and sauté for a minute.
4. Remove pan from heat and let it cool for 5 minutes.
5. Pour melted butter over chicken and potatoes. Sprinkle with pepper and parsley.
6. Set to bake at 400 F for 25 minutes. After 5 minutes place the casserole dish in the preheated oven.
7. Remove the casserole dish from the oven. Sprinkle mozzarella cheese and cheddar cheese on top of chicken and potatoes and bake for 5 minutes more.
8. Serve and enjoy.

Nutritional Value (Amount per Serving):

- Calories 635
- Fat 40 g
- Carbohydrates 16.8 g
- Sugar 0.3 g
- Protein 51.6 g
- Cholesterol 210 mg

Baked Spinach Cheese Chicken

Preparation Time: 10 minutes
Cooking Time: 20 minutes
Serve: 2

Ingredients:

- 2 chicken breasts, boneless & skinless
- 1/2 tsp garlic powder
- 1/4 cup sun-dried tomatoes, chopped
- 1/4 cup cheddar cheese, shredded
- 3 oz cream cheese
- 2 cups fresh spinach, chopped
- 3/4 tsp pepper
- 3/4 tsp salt

Directions:

1. Fit the Cuisinart oven with the rack in position 1.
2. Slice the chicken breasts into the half and place them into the baking dish. Season with pepper and salt.
3. Cook spinach in the pan until wilted.
4. In a bowl, mix spinach, garlic powder, tomatoes, cheddar cheese, and cream cheese.
5. Spread spinach mixture on top of chicken breasts.
6. Set to bake at 425 F for 25 minutes. After 5 minutes place the baking dish in the preheated oven.
7. Serve and enjoy.

Nutritional Value (Amount per Serving):

- Calories 498
- Fat 30.5 g
- Carbohydrates 4.3 g
- Sugar 1.1 g
- Protein 50.2 g
- Cholesterol 192 mg

Honey Chicken Wings

Preparation Time: 10 minutes
Cooking Time: 15 minutes
Serve: 2

Ingredients:
- 2 chicken drumsticks
- 2 tsp honey
- 2 tsp olive oil
- 2 garlic cloves, minced

Directions:
1. Fit the Cuisinart oven with the rack in position 2.
2. In a bowl, mix honey, garlic, and olive oil.
3. Add chicken drumsticks and coat well and let it sit for 20 minutes.
4. Arrange chicken drumsticks in the air fryer basket then place an air fryer basket in the baking pan.
5. Place a baking pan on the oven rack. Set to air fry at 400 F for 15 minutes.
6. Serve and enjoy.

Nutritional Value (Amount per Serving):
- Calories 143
- Fat 7.3 g
- Carbohydrates 6.8 g
- Sugar 5.8 g
- Protein 12.9 g
- Cholesterol 40 mg

Baked Zucchini Chicken Tenders

Preparation Time: 10 minutes

Cooking Time: 30 minutes

Serve: 4

Ingredients:
- 2 lbs chicken tenders
- 1 large zucchini
- 2 tbsp feta cheese, crumbled
- 1 tbsp fresh lemon juice
- 1 tbsp fresh dill, chopped
- 1 cup grape tomatoes
- 2 tbsp olive oil

Directions:
1. Fit the Cuisinart oven with the rack in position 1.
2. Coat chicken with oil and place in baking pan along with zucchini, dill, and tomatoes. Season with salt.
3. Set to bake at 400 F for 35 minutes. After 5 minutes place the baking dish in the preheated oven.
4. Drizzle with lemon juice and top with feta cheese.
5. Serve and enjoy.

Nutritional Value (Amount per Serving):
- Calories 527
- Fat 25.1 g
- Carbohydrates 5.2 g
- Sugar 2.9 g
- Protein 67.9 g
- Cholesterol 206 mg

Simple Jerk Chicken Wings

Preparation Time: 10 minutes

Cooking Time: 20 minutes

Serve: 2

Ingredients:

- 1 lb chicken wings
- 1 tbsp jerk seasoning
- 1 tsp olive oil
- 1 tbsp cornstarch
- Pepper
- Salt

Directions:

1. Fit the Cuisinart oven with the rack in position 2.
2. In a large bowl, add chicken wings.
3. Add remaining ingredients on top of chicken wings and toss to coat.
4. Add chicken wings to the air fryer basket then place an air fryer basket in the baking pan.
5. Place a baking pan on the oven rack. Set to air fry at 380 F for 20 minutes.
6. Serve and enjoy.

Nutritional Value (Amount per Serving):

- Calories 466
- Fat 19.1 g
- Carbohydrates 3.7 g
- Sugar 0 g
- Protein 65.6 g
- Cholesterol 202 mg

Cracker Apple Chicken

Preparation Time: 10 minutes

Cooking Time: 45 minutes

Serve: 2

Ingredients:

- 2 chicken breasts, skinless and boneless
- 1 apple, sliced
- 12 Ritz cracker, crushed
- 10 oz can condensed cheddar cheese soup
- Pepper
- Salt

Directions:

1. Fit the Cuisinart oven with the rack in position 1.
2. Season chicken with pepper and salt and place into the baking dish.
3. Arrange sliced apple on top of chicken.
4. Sprinkle crushed crackers on top.
5. Set to bake at 350 F for 50 minutes. After 5 minutes place the baking dish in the preheated oven.
6. Pour cheddar cheese soup on top and serve.

Nutritional Value (Amount per Serving):

- Calories 924
- Fat 38.2 g
- Carbohydrates 87 g
- Sugar 21.4 g
- Protein 51.8 g
- Cholesterol 136 mg

Meatballs

Preparation Time: 10 minutes
Cooking Time: 20 minutes
Serve: 4

Ingredients:

- 1 lb ground turkey
- 1/4 cup basil, chopped
- 3 tbsp scallions, chopped
- 1 egg, lightly beaten
- 1/2 cup almond flour
- 1/2 tsp red pepper, crushed
- 1 tbsp lemongrass, chopped
- 1 1/2 tbsp fish sauce
- 2 garlic cloves, minced

Directions:

1. Fit the Cuisinart oven with the rack in position 2.
2. Line the air fryer basket with parchment paper.
3. Add all ingredients into a large bowl and mix until well combined.
4. Make small balls from meat mixture and place in the air fryer basket then place the air fryer basket in the baking pan.
5. Place a baking pan on the oven rack. Set to air fry at 380 F for 20 minutes.
6. Serve and enjoy.

Nutritional Value (Amount per Serving):

- Calories 269
- Fat 15.4 g
- Carbohydrates 3.4 g
- Sugar 1.3 g
- Protein 33.9 g
- Cholesterol 157 mg

Sweet & Spicy Chicken Wings

Preparation Time: 10 minutes

Cooking Time: 30 minutes

Serve: 4

Ingredients:

- 12 chicken wings
- 1/2 cup hot sauce
- 1/2 cup honey
- Pepper
- Salt

Directions:

1. Fit the Cuisinart oven with the rack in position 2.
2. Season chicken wings with pepper and salt.
3. Arrange chicken wings in the air fryer basket then place an air fryer basket in the baking pan.
4. Place a baking pan on the oven rack. Set to air fry at 400 F for 25 minutes.
5. Meanwhile, add honey and hot sauce in a saucepan and heat over medium heat for 5 minutes.
6. Add chicken wings in a bowl. Pour
7. sauce over chicken wings and toss well.
8. Serve and enjoy.

Nutritional Value (Amount per Serving):

- Calories 698
- Fat 22.2 g
- Carbohydrates 35.4 g
- Sugar 35.2 g
- Protein 89.4 g
- Cholesterol 256 mg

Air Fryer Chicken Tenders

Preparation Time: 10 minutes

Cooking Time: 16 minutes

Serve: 4

Ingredients:

- 1 lb chicken tenders
- For rub:
- 1/2 tbsp dried thyme
- 1 tbsp garlic powder
- 1 tbsp paprika
- 1/2 tbsp onion powder
- 1/2 tsp cayenne pepper
- Pepper
- Salt

Directions:

1. Fit the Cuisinart oven with the rack in position 2.
2. In a bowl, add all rub ingredients and mix well.
3. Add chicken tenders into the bowl and coat well.
4. Place chicken tenders in the air fryer basket then place an air fryer basket in the baking pan.
5. Place a baking pan on the oven rack. Set to air fry at 370 F for 16 minutes.
6. Serve and enjoy.

Nutritional Value (Amount per Serving):

- Calories 232
- Fat 8.7 g
- Carbohydrates 3.6 g
- Sugar 1 g
- Protein 33.6 g
- Cholesterol 101 mg

Easy BBQ Chicken Drumsticks

Preparation Time: 10 minutes
Cooking Time: 25 minutes
Serve: 4

Ingredients:

- 4 chicken drumsticks
- 1/4 tsp paprika
- 1/2 tsp garlic powder
- 2 tbsp olive oil
- 1/2 cup BBQ sauce
- 1/2 tsp onion powder
- Pepper
- Salt

Directions:

1. Fit the Cuisinart oven with the rack in position 2.
2. In a mixing bowl, add chicken drumsticks, onion powder, garlic powder, olive oil, paprika, pepper, and salt and toss well.
3. Add chicken drumsticks to the air fryer basket then place an air fryer basket in baking pan.
4. Place a baking pan on the oven rack. Set to air fry at 400 F for 20 minutes.
5. Brush chicken drumsticks with BBQ sauce and air fry for 5 minutes.
6. Serve and enjoy.

Nutritional Value (Amount per Serving):

- Calories 187
- Fat 9.7 g
- Carbohydrates 11.9 g
- Sugar 8.4 g
- Protein 12.8 g
- Cholesterol 40 mg

Greek Chicken Breast

Preparation Time: 10 minutes

Cooking Time: 25 minutes

Serve: 4

Ingredients:

- 4 chicken breasts, skinless & boneless
- 1 tbsp olive oil

For rub:

- 1 tsp oregano
- 1 tsp thyme
- 1 tsp parsley
- 1 tsp onion powder
- 1 tsp basil
- Pepper
- Salt

Directions:

1. Fit the Cuisinart oven with the rack in position 2.
2. Brush chicken with olive oil.
3. In a small bowl, mix together all rub ingredients and rub all over the chicken breasts.
4. Place chicken into the air fryer basket then places the air fryer basket in the baking pan.
5. Place a baking pan on the oven rack. Set to air fry at 390 F for 25 minutes.
6. Serve and enjoy.

Nutritional Value (Amount per Serving):

- Calories 312
- Fat 14.4 g
- Carbohydrates 0.9 g
- Sugar 0.2 g
- Protein 42.4 g
- Cholesterol 130 mg

Chapter 4: Beef, Pork & Lamb

Stuffed Pork Chops

Preparation Time: 10 minutes
Cooking Time: 35 minutes
Serve: 4

Ingredients:

- 4 pork chops, boneless and thick-cut
- 2 tbsp olives, chopped
- 3 tbsp sun-dried tomatoes, chopped
- 1/2 cup goat cheese, crumbled
- 3 garlic cloves, minced
- 2 tbsp fresh parsley, chopped

Directions:

1. Fit the Cuisinart oven with the rack in position 1.
2. In a bowl, combine together cheese, garlic, parsley, olives, and sun-dried tomatoes.
3. Stuff cheese mixture all the pork chops.
4. Season pork chops with pepper and salt and place in baking pan.
5. Set to bake at 375 F for 40 minutes. After 5 minutes place the baking pan in the preheated oven.
6. Serve and enjoy.

Nutritional Value (Amount per Serving):

- Calories 295
- Fat 22.6 g
- Carbohydrates 1.6 g
- Sugar 0.4 g
- Protein 20.2 g
- Cholesterol 75 mg

Spicy Meatballs

Preparation Time: 10 minutes
Cooking Time: 30 minutes
Serve: 4

Ingredients:

- 1 lb ground beef
- 4 oz cream cheese
- 1 tsp dried basil
- 2 tbsp Worcestershire sauce
- 1/3 cup milk
- 1/2 cup cheddar cheese, shredded
- 3/4 cup breadcrumbs
- 2 jalapenos, minced
- 1/2 onion, minced
- 1 tsp salt

Directions:

1. Fit the Cuisinart oven with the rack in position 1.
2. Add all ingredients into the mixing bowl and mix until well combined.
3. Make small balls from the meat mixture and place it into the parchment-lined baking pan.
4. Set to bake at 400 F for 35 minutes. After 5 minutes place the baking pan in the preheated oven.
5. Serve and enjoy.

Nutritional Value (Amount per Serving):

- Calories 472
- Fat 23.2 g
- Carbohydrates 19.7 g
- Sugar 4.6 g
- Protein 43.7 g
- Cholesterol 149 mg

Perfect Beef Hash brown Bake

Preparation Time: 10 minutes

Cooking Time: 40 minutes

Serve: 4

Ingredients:

- 1 lb ground beef
- 2 cups cheddar cheese, shredded
- 1 cup milk
- 10 oz can cream of mushroom soup
- 30 oz frozen shredded hash browns
- 1 tsp garlic powder
- 1 tbsp onion, minced
- Pepper
- Salt

Directions:

1. Fit the Cuisinart oven with the rack in position 1.
2. In a pan, brown ground beef with garlic powder, onion, pepper, and salt. Drain.
3. In a bowl, mix meat, shredded cheese, milk, soup, and hash browns.
4. Pour meat mixture into the greased 9*13-inch baking dish.
5. Set to bake at 350 F for 45 minutes. After 5 minutes place the baking dish in the preheated oven.
6. Serve and enjoy.

Nutritional Value (Amount per Serving):

- Calories 514
- Fat 28.3 g
- Carbohydrates 11.4 g
- Sugar 4.8 g
- Protein 51.6 g
- Cholesterol 168 mg

Curried Beef Patties

Preparation Time: 10 minutes

Cooking Time: 25 minutes

Serve: 6

Ingredients:

- 1 lb ground beef
- 2 eggs, lightly beaten
- 1/2 onion, chopped
- 2 medium zucchini, grated and squeeze out all liquid
- 1/2 tsp chili powder
- 1 tsp curry powder
- 1 cup breadcrumbs
- Pepper
- Salt

Directions:

1. Fit the Cuisinart oven with the rack in position 1.
2. Add all ingredients into the large bowl and mix until well combined.
3. Make small patties from the meat mixture and place it into the baking pan.
4. Set to bake at 400 F for 30 minutes. After 5 minutes place the baking pan in the preheated oven.
5. Serve and enjoy.

Nutritional Value (Amount per Serving):

- Calories 248
- Fat 7.3 g
- Carbohydrates 16.4 g
- Sugar 2.8 g
- Protein 28.1 g
- Cholesterol 122 mg

Flavorful Sirloin Steak

Preparation Time: 10 minutes
Cooking Time: 14 minutes
Serve: 2

Ingredients:

- 1 lb sirloin steaks
- 1/2 tsp garlic powder
- 1/2 tsp onion powder
- 1/4 tsp smoked paprika
- 1 tsp olive oil
- Pepper
- Salt

Directions:

1. Fit the Cuisinart oven with the rack in position 2.
2. Line the air fryer basket with parchment paper.
3. Brush steak with olive oil and rub with garlic powder, onion powder, paprika, pepper, and salt.
4. Place the steak in the air fryer basket then places an air fryer basket in the baking pan.
5. Place a baking pan on the oven rack. Set to air fry at 400 F for 14 minutes.
6. Serve and enjoy.

Nutritional Value (Amount per Serving):

- Calories 447
- Fat 16.5 g
- Carbohydrates 1.2 g
- Sugar 0.4 g
- Protein 69 g
- Cholesterol 203 mg

Meatballs

Preparation Time: 10 minutes
Cooking Time: 20 minutes
Serve: 4

Ingredients:

- 1 lb ground beef
- 1/2 cup kale, chopped
- 2 garlic cloves, finely chopped
- 1/2 onion, finely chopped
- 4 oz mushrooms, finely chopped
- 3/4 cup cooked quinoa
- 2 tsp Italian seasoning
- 1/4 cup rolled oats
- 1 egg, lightly beaten
- Pepper
- Salt

Directions:

1. Fit the Cuisinart oven with the rack in position 2.
2. Line the air fryer basket with parchment paper.
3. Add all ingredients into a large bowl and mix until well combined.
4. Make small balls from meat mixture and place in the air fryer basket then place the air fryer basket in the baking pan.
5. Place a baking pan on the oven rack. Set to air fry at 380 F for 20 minutes.
6. Serve and enjoy.

Nutritional Value (Amount per Serving):

- Calories 388
- Fat 11.2 g
- Carbohydrates 27.9 g
- Sugar 1.4 g
- Protein 42.4 g
- Cholesterol 144 mg

Delicious Pork Belly

Preparation Time: 10 minutes
Cooking Time: 55 minutes
Serve: 6

Ingredients:

- 3 lbs pork belly, cut into 2-inch cubes
- 3 green onions stalk, chopped
- 1/4 tsp pepper
- 1 tbsp sesame oil
- 2 tbsp brown sugar
- 1/4 cup rice vinegar
- 1/4 cup soy sauce
- 1 tsp red chili flakes
- 1 tsp garlic, minced
- 1/4 tsp salt

Directions:

1. Fit the Cuisinart oven with the rack in position 1.
2. Add all ingredients into the zip-lock bag, seal bag shake well and place in the refrigerator for 1 hour.
3. Place marinated pork belly cubes into the parchment-lined baking pan.
4. Set to bake at 400 F for 60 minutes. After 5 minutes place the baking pan in the preheated oven.
5. Turn pork belly cubes after 30 minutes.
6. Serve and enjoy.

Nutritional Value (Amount per Serving):

- Calories 362
- Fat 32.3 g
- Carbohydrates 5.5 g
- Sugar 3.3 g
- Protein 10.4 g
- Cholesterol 51 mg

Ranch Pork Chops

Preparation Time: 10 minutes

Cooking Time: 35 minutes

Serve: 6

Ingredients:

- 6 pork chops, boneless
- 1 tsp dried parsley
- 2 tbsp dry ranch mix
- 1/4 cup olive oil

Directions:

1. Fit the Cuisinart oven with the rack in position 1.
2. Place pork chops in baking dish.
3. Mix together remaining ingredients and pour over pork chops.
4. Set to bake at 425 F for 40 minutes. After 5 minutes place the baking dish in the preheated oven.
5. Serve and enjoy.

Nutritional Value (Amount per Serving):

- Calories 330
- Fat 28.3 g
- Carbohydrates 0.4 g
- Sugar 0 g
- Protein 18 g
- Cholesterol 69 mg

Meatballs

Preparation Time: 10 minutes
Cooking Time: 20 minutes
Serve: 4

Ingredients:

- 1 egg, lightly beaten
- 1 lb ground lamb
- 2 tbsp fresh parsley, chopped
- 1 tbsp garlic, minced
- 1/4 tsp red pepper flakes
- 1 tsp ground cumin
- 2 tsp fresh oregano, chopped
- 1/4 tsp pepper
- 1 tsp kosher salt

Directions:

1. Fit the Cuisinart oven with the rack in position 1.
2. Add all ingredients into the mixing bowl and mix until well combined.
3. Make small balls from meat mixture and place onto the parchment-lined baking pan.
4. Set to bake at 425 F for 25 minutes. After 5 minutes place the baking pan in the preheated oven.
5. Serve and enjoy.

Nutritional Value (Amount per Serving):

- Calories 235
- Fat 9.7 g
- Carbohydrates 1.7 g
- Sugar 0.2 g
- Protein 33.6 g
- Cholesterol 143 mg

Baked Pork Tenderloin

Preparation Time: 10 minutes

Cooking Time: 35 minutes

Serve: 6

Ingredients:

- 2 lbs pork tenderloin
- 3 garlic cloves, chopped
- Pepper
- Salt

For the spice mix:

- 1/4 tsp chili powder
- 1/4 tsp cayenne
- 1 tsp cinnamon
- 1 tsp cumin
- 1 tsp coriander
- 1 tsp oregano
- 1/4 tsp cloves

Directions:

1. Fit the Cuisinart oven with the rack in position 1.
2. In a small bowl, mix all spice ingredients and set aside.
3. Using a sharp knife make slits on pork tenderloin and insert garlic into each slit.
4. Rub spice mixture over pork tenderloin.
5. Place pork tenderloin in baking pan.
6. Set to bake at 375 F for 40 minutes. After 5 minutes place the baking pan in the preheated oven.
7. Slice and serve.

Nutritional Value (Amount per Serving):

- Calories 222
- Fat 5.5 g
- Carbohydrates 1.3 g
- Sugar 0.1 g
- Protein 39.8 g
- Cholesterol 110 mg

Tasty Steak Tips

Preparation Time: 10 minutes

Cooking Time: 5 minutes

Serve: 4

Ingredients:

- 1 lb steak, cut into cubes
- 1 tsp olive oil
- 1/4 tsp garlic powder
- 1 tsp Montreal steak seasoning
- Pepper
- Salt

Directions:

1. Fit the Cuisinart oven with the rack in position 2.
2. In a bowl, add steak cubes and remaining ingredients and toss well.
3. Add marinated steak cubes to the air fryer basket then place an air fryer basket in the baking pan.
4. Place a baking pan on the oven rack. Set to air fry at 400 F for 5 minutes.
5. Serve and enjoy.

Nutritional Value (Amount per Serving):

- Calories 236
- Fat 6.8 g
- Carbohydrates 0.2 g
- Sugar 0 g
- Protein 41 g
- Cholesterol 102 mg

Spiced Pork Chops

Preparation Time: 10 minutes

Cooking Time: 16 minutes

Serve: 4

Ingredients:

- 4 pork chops, boneless
- 1/2 tsp granulated onion
- 1/2 tsp granulated garlic
- 1/4 tsp sugar
- 2 tsp olive oil
- 1/2 tsp celery seed
- 1/2 tsp parsley
- 1/2 tsp salt

Directions:

1. Fit the Cuisinart oven with the rack in position 2.
2. Brush pork chops with olive oil.
3. Mix celery seed, parsley, granulated onion, garlic, sugar, and salt and sprinkle over pork chops.
4. Place pork chops in the air fryer basket then place an air fryer basket in the baking pan.
5. Place a baking pan on the oven rack. Set to air fry at 350 F for 16 minutes.
6. Serve and enjoy.

Nutritional Value (Amount per Serving):

- Calories 279
- Fat 22.3 g
- Carbohydrates 0.6 g
- Sugar 0.3 g
- Protein 18.1 g
- Cholesterol 69 mg

Ranch Beef Patties

Preparation Time: 10 minutes
Cooking Time: 12 minutes
Serve: 4

Ingredients:

- 1 lb ground beef
- 1/2 tsp onion powder
- 1/2 tsp garlic powder
- 2 tsp dried parsley
- 1/8 tsp dried dill
- 1/2 tsp paprika
- 1/2 tsp dried dill
- Pepper
- Salt

Directions:

1. Fit the Cuisinart oven with the rack in position 2.
2. Line the air fryer basket with parchment paper.
3. Add all ingredients into the large bowl and mix until well combined.
4. Make four even shape patties from the meat mixture and place in the air fryer basket then place an air fryer basket in the baking pan.
5. Place a baking pan on the oven rack. Set to air fry at 350 F for 12 minutes.
6. Serve and enjoy.

Nutritional Value (Amount per Serving):

- Calories 214
- Fat 7.1 g
- Carbohydrates 0.8 g
- Sugar 0.2 g
- Protein 34.6 g
- Cholesterol 101 mg

Delicious Air Fryer Kebabs

Preparation Time: 10 minutes

Cooking Time: 15 minutes

Serve: 4

Ingredients:

- 1 lb ground beef
- 1/4 cup cilantro, chopped
- 1/2 cup onion, minced
- 1/4 tsp ground cinnamon
- 1/2 tsp turmeric
- 1 tbsp ginger garlic paste
- 1/4 tsp ground cardamom
- 1/2 tsp cayenne
- 1 tsp salt

Directions:

1. Fit the Cuisinart oven with the rack in position 2.
2. Add meat and remaining ingredients into the large bowl and mix until well combined.
3. Make sausage shape kebabs and place them in an air fryer basket then place an air fryer basket in the baking pan.
4. Place a baking pan on the oven rack. Set to air fry at 350 F for 15 minutes.
5. Serve and enjoy.

Nutritional Value (Amount per Serving):

- Calories 219
- Fat 7.2 g
- Carbohydrates 1.9 g
- Sugar 0.7 g
- Protein 34.7 g
- Cholesterol 101 mg

Honey Garlic Pork Chops

Preparation Time: 10 minutes

Cooking Time: 12 minutes

Serve: 4

Ingredients:

- 4 pork chops
- 2 tbsp lemon juice
- 1/4 cup honey
- 2 garlic cloves, minced
- 1 tbsp olive oil
- 1 tbsp sweet chili sauce
- Pepper
- Salt

Directions:

1. Fit the Cuisinart oven with the rack in position 2.
2. Season pork chops with pepper and salt and place in air fryer basket then place air fryer basket in baking pan.
3. Place a baking pan on the oven rack. Set to air fry at 400 F for 12 minutes.
4. Meanwhile, heat oil in a pan over medium heat.
5. Add garlic and sauté for 30 seconds.
6. Add remaining ingredients and stir well and cook for 3 minutes.
7. Place pork chops on serving dish.
8. Pour sauce over pork chops and serve.

Nutritional Value (Amount per Serving):

- Calories 362
- Fat 23.5 g
- Carbohydrates 19.6 g
- Sugar 19.1 g
- Protein 18.2 g
- Cholesterol 69 mg

Chapter 5: Fish & Seafood

Spicy Halibut

Preparation Time: 10 minutes
Cooking Time: 12 minutes
Serve: 4

Ingredients:

- 1 lb halibut fillets
- 1/2 tsp chili powder
- 1/2 tsp smoked paprika
- 1/4 cup olive oil
- 1/4 tsp garlic powder
- Pepper
- Salt

Directions:

1. Fit the Cuisinart oven with the rack in position 1.
2. Place halibut fillets in a baking dish.
3. In a small bowl, mix oil, garlic powder, paprika, pepper, chili powder, and salt.
4. Brush fish fillets with oil mixture.
5. Set to bake at 425 F for 17 minutes. After 5 minutes place the baking dish in the preheated oven.
6. Serve and enjoy.

Nutritional Value (Amount per Serving):

- Calories 236
- Fat 15.3 g
- Carbohydrates 0.5 g
- Sugar 0.1 g
- Protein 24 g
- Cholesterol 36 mg

Basil Tomato Salmon

Preparation Time: 10 minutes
Cooking Time: 20 minutes
Serve: 2

Ingredients:
- 2 salmon fillets
- 1 tomato, sliced
- 1 tbsp dried basil
- 2 tbsp parmesan cheese, grated
- 1 tbsp olive oil

Directions:
1. Fit the Cuisinart oven with the rack in position 1.
2. Place salmon fillets in a baking dish.
3. Sprinkle basil on top of salmon fillets.
4. Arrange tomato slices on top of salmon fillets. Drizzle with oil and top with cheese.
5. Set to bake at 375 F for 25 minutes. After 5 minutes place the baking dish in the preheated oven.
6. Serve and enjoy.

Nutritional Value (Amount per Serving):
- Calories 324
- Fat 19.6 g
- Carbohydrates 1.5 g
- Sugar 0.8 g
- Protein 37.1 g
- Cholesterol 83 mg

Easy Blackened Shrimp

Preparation Time: 10 minutes

Cooking Time: 10 minutes

Serve: 6

Ingredients:

- 1 lb shrimp, deveined
- 1 tbsp olive oil
- 1/4 tsp pepper
- 2 tsp blackened seasoning
- 1/4 tsp salt

Directions:

1. Fit the Cuisinart oven with the rack in position 1.
2. Toss shrimp with oil, pepper, blackened seasoning, and salt.
3. Transfer shrimp into the baking pan.
4. Set to bake at 400 F for 15 minutes. After 5 minutes place the baking pan in the preheated oven.
5. Serve and enjoy.

Nutritional Value (Amount per Serving):

- Calories 167
- Fat 4.3 g
- Carbohydrates 10.5 g
- Sugar 0 g
- Protein 20.6 g
- Cholesterol 159 mg

Lemon Butter Shrimp

Preparation Time: 10 minutes

Cooking Time: 12 minutes

Serve: 4

Ingredients:

- 1 1/4 lbs shrimp, peeled & deveined
- 2 tbsp fresh parsley, chopped
- 2 tbsp fresh lemon juice
- 1 tbsp garlic, minced
- 1/4 cup butter
- Pepper
- Salt

Directions:

1. Fit the Cuisinart oven with the rack in position 1.
2. Add shrimp into the baking dish.
3. Melt butter in a pan over low heat. Add garlic and sauté for 30 seconds. Stir in lemon juice.
4. Pour melted butter mixture over shrimp. Season with pepper and salt.
5. Set to bake at 350 F for 17 minutes. After 5 minutes place the baking dish in the preheated oven.
6. Garnish with parsley and serve.

Nutritional Value (Amount per Serving):

- Calories 276
- Fat 14 g
- Carbohydrates 3.2 g
- Sugar 0.2 g
- Protein 32.7 g
- Cholesterol 329 mg

Tender & Juicy Cajun Cod

Preparation Time: 10 minutes

Cooking Time: 15 minutes

Serve: 6

Ingredients:

- 3 cod fillets, cut in half
- 1 tbsp Cajun seasoning
- 1 tbsp garlic, minced
- 1 tbsp olive oil
- 1/4 cup butter, melted
- Pepper
- Salt

Directions:

1. Fit the Cuisinart oven with the rack in position 1.
2. Season fish fillets with pepper and salt and place in a 9*13-inch baking dish.
3. Mix together the remaining ingredients and pour over fish fillets.
4. Set to bake at 400 F for 20 minutes. After 5 minutes place the baking dish in the preheated oven.
5. Serve and enjoy.

Nutritional Value (Amount per Serving):

- Calories 126
- Fat 10.4 g
- Carbohydrates 0.5 g
- Sugar 0 g
- Protein 8.2 g
- Cholesterol 42 mg

Spicy Baked Shrimp

Preparation Time: 10 minutes

Cooking Time: 8 minutes

Serve: 4

Ingredients:

- 2 lbs shrimp, peeled & deveined
- 1/4 tsp cayenne pepper
- 1 tsp garlic powder
- 2 tbsp chili powder
- 2 tbsp olive oil
- 1 tsp kosher salt

Directions:

1. Fit the Cuisinart oven with the rack in position 1.
2. Toss shrimp with remaining ingredients.
3. Transfer shrimp into the baking pan.
4. Set to bake at 400 F for 13 minutes. After 5 minutes place the baking pan in the preheated oven.
5. Serve and enjoy.

Nutritional Value (Amount per Serving):

- Calories 344
- Fat 11.5 g
- Carbohydrates 6.1 g
- Sugar 0.5 g
- Protein 52.3 g
- Cholesterol 478 mg

Spicy Catfish

Preparation Time: 10 minutes
Cooking Time: 15 minutes
Serve: 4

Ingredients:

- 1 lb catfish fillets, cut 1/2-inch thick
- 1 tsp crushed red pepper
- 2 tsp onion powder
- 1 tbsp dried oregano, crushed
- 1/2 tsp ground cumin
- 1/2 tsp chili powder
- Pepper
- Salt

Directions:

1. Fit the Cuisinart oven with the rack in position 1.
2. In a small bowl, mix cumin, chili powder, crushed red pepper, onion powder, oregano, pepper, and salt.
3. Rub fish fillets with the spice mixture and place in baking dish.
4. Set to bake at 350 F for 20 minutes. After 5 minutes place the baking dish in the preheated oven.
5. Serve and enjoy.

Nutritional Value (Amount per Serving):

- Calories 164
- Fat 8.9 g
- Carbohydrates 2.3 g
- Sugar 0.6 g
- Protein 18 g
- Cholesterol 53 mg

Greek Cod with Asparagus

Preparation Time: 10 minutes

Cooking Time: 20 minutes

Serve: 2

Ingredients:

- 1 lb cod, cut into 4 pieces
- 8 asparagus spears
- 1 leek, sliced
- 1 onion, quartered
- 2 tomatoes, halved
- 1/2 tsp oregano
- 1/2 tsp red chili flakes
- 1/2 cup olives, chopped
- 2 tbsp olive oil
- 1/4 tsp pepper
- 1/4 tsp salt

Directions:

1. Fit the Cuisinart oven with the rack in position 1.
2. Arrange fish pieces, olives, asparagus, leek, onion, and tomatoes in a baking dish.
3. Season with oregano, chili flakes, pepper, and salt and drizzle with olive oil.
4. Set to bake at 400 F for 25 minutes. After 5 minutes place the baking dish in the preheated oven.
5. Serve and enjoy.

Nutritional Value (Amount per Serving):

- Calories 489
- Fat 20.2 g
- Carbohydrates 22.5 g
- Sugar 9.1 g
- Protein 56.6 g
- Cholesterol 125 mg

Perfect Crab Cakes

Preparation Time: 10 minutes

Cooking Time: 30 minutes

Serve: 6

Ingredients:

- 16 oz lump crab meat
- 1/4 cup celery, diced
- 1/4 cup onion, diced
- 1 cup crushed crackers
- 1 tsp old bay seasoning
- 1 tsp brown mustard
- 2/3 cup mashed avocado

Directions:

1. Fit the Cuisinart oven with the rack in position 1.
2. Add all ingredients into the bowl and mix until just combined.
3. Make small patties from mixture and place in parchment-lined baking pan.
4. Set to bake at 350 F for 35 minutes. After 5 minutes place the baking dish in the preheated oven.
5. Serve and enjoy.

Nutritional Value (Amount per Serving):

- Calories 84
- Fat 7.7 g
- Carbohydrates 4.6 g
- Sugar 0.8 g
- Protein 11.5 g
- Cholesterol 43 mg

Dijon Salmon Fillets

Preparation Time: 10 minutes
Cooking Time: 15 minutes
Serve: 4

Ingredients:

- 1 lb salmon fillets
- 2 tbsp Dijon mustard
- 1/4 cup brown sugar
- Pepper
- Salt

Directions:

1. Fit the Cuisinart oven with the rack in position 2.
2. Season salmon fillets with pepper and salt.
3. In a small bowl, mix Dijon mustard and brown sugar.
4. Brush salmon fillets with Dijon mustard mixture.
5. Place salmon fillets in the air fryer basket then place an air fryer basket in the baking pan.
6. Place a baking pan on the oven rack. Set to air fry at 350 F for 15 minutes.
7. Serve and enjoy.

Nutritional Value (Amount per Serving):

- Calories 190
- Fat 7.3 g
- Carbohydrates 9.3 g
- Sugar 8.9 g
- Protein 22.4 g
- Cholesterol 50 mg

Air Fry Prawns

Preparation Time: 10 minutes

Cooking Time: 6 minutes

Serve: 4

Ingredients:

- 24 prawns
- 6 tbsp mayonnaise
- 1 1/2 tsp chili powder
- 2 tbsp vinegar
- 2 tbsp ketchup
- 1 tsp red chili flakes
- 1/2 tsp sea salt

Directions:

1. Fit the Cuisinart oven with the rack in position 2.
2. In a bowl, toss prawns with chili flakes, chili powder, and salt.
3. Add shrimp to the air fryer basket then place an air fryer basket in the baking pan.
4. Place a baking pan on the oven rack. Set to air fry at 350 F for 6 minutes.
5. In a small bowl, mix mayonnaise, vinegar, and ketchup and serve with shrimp.

Nutritional Value (Amount per Serving):

- Calories 255
- Fat 9.8 g
- Carbohydrates 9.8 g
- Sugar 3.2 g
- Protein 30.5 g
- Cholesterol 284 mg

Miso White Fish Fillets

Preparation Time: 10 minutes

Cooking Time: 10 minutes

Serve: 2

Ingredients:

- 2 cod fish fillets
- 2 tbsp brown sugar
- 2 tbsp miso
- 1 tbsp garlic, chopped

Directions:

1. Fit the Cuisinart oven with the rack in position 2.
2. Add all ingredients to the zip-lock bag and marinate fish in the refrigerator overnight.
3. Place marinated fish fillets in the air fryer basket then place an air fryer basket in the baking pan.
4. Place a baking pan on the oven rack. Set to air fry at 350 F for 10 minutes.
5. Serve and enjoy.

Nutritional Value (Amount per Serving):

- Calories 9
- Fat 0.1 g
- Carbohydrates 0.5 g
- Sugar 0.3 g
- Protein 1.5 g
- Cholesterol 3 mg

Rosemary Garlic Shrimp

Preparation Time: 10 minutes

Cooking Time: 10 minutes

Serve: 4

Ingredients:

- 1 lb shrimp, peeled and deveined
- 2 garlic cloves, minced
- 1/2 tbsp fresh rosemary, chopped
- 1 tbsp olive oil
- Pepper
- Salt

Directions:

1. Fit the Cuisinart oven with the rack in position 1.
2. Add shrimp and remaining ingredients in a large bowl and toss well.
3. Pour shrimp mixture into the baking dish.
4. Set to bake at 400 F for 15 minutes. After 5 minutes place the baking dish in the preheated oven.
5. Serve and enjoy.

Nutritional Value (Amount per Serving):

- Calories 168
- Fat 5.5 g
- Carbohydrates 2.5 g
- Sugar 0 g
- Protein 26 g
- Cholesterol 239 mg

Italian Cod

Preparation Time: 10 minutes

Cooking Time: 20 minutes

Serve: 4

Ingredients:

- 1 1/2 lbs cod fillet
- 1/4 cup olives, sliced
- 1 lb cherry tomatoes, halved
- 2 garlic cloves, crushed
- 1 small onion, chopped
- 1 tbsp olive oil
- 1/4 cup of water
- 1 tsp Italian seasoning
- Pepper
- Salt

Directions:

1. Fit the Cuisinart oven with the rack in position 1.
2. Place fish fillets, olives, tomatoes, garlic, and onion in a baking dish. Drizzle with oil.
3. Sprinkle with Italian seasoning, pepper, and salt. Pour water into the dish.
4. Set to bake at 400 F for 25 minutes. After 5 minutes place the baking dish in the preheated oven.
5. Serve and enjoy.

Nutritional Value (Amount per Serving):

- Calories 210
- Fat 6.5 g
- Carbohydrates 7.2 g
- Sugar 3.8 g
- Protein 31.7 g
- Cholesterol 84 mg

Air Fry Tuna Patties

Preparation Time: 10 minutes
Cooking Time: 6 minutes
Serve: 4

Ingredients:
- 1 egg, lightly beaten
- 8 oz can tuna, drained
- 1/4 cup breadcrumbs
- 1 tbsp mustard
- 1/4 tsp garlic powder
- Pepper
- Salt

Directions:
1. Fit the Cuisinart oven with the rack in position 2.
2. Add all ingredients into the large bowl and mix until well combined.
3. Make four equal shapes of patties from the mixture and place in the air fryer basket then place an air fryer basket in the baking pan.
4. Place a baking pan on the oven rack. Set to air fry at 400 F for 6 minutes.
5. Serve and enjoy.

Nutritional Value (Amount per Serving):
- Calories 122
- Fat 2.7 g
- Carbohydrates 6.1 g
- Sugar 0.7 g
- Protein 17.5 g
- Cholesterol 58 mg

Chapter 6: Vegetables & Side Dishes

Baked Vegetables

Preparation Time: 10 minutes
Cooking Time: 30 minutes
Serve: 6

Ingredients:

- 2 zucchini, sliced
- 2 tomatoes, quartered
- 6 fresh basil leaves, sliced
- 2 tsp Italian seasoning
- 2 tbsp olive oil
- 1 eggplant, sliced
- 1 onion, sliced
- 1 bell pepper, cut into strips
- Pepper
- Salt

Directions:

1. Fit the Cuisinart oven with the rack in position 1.
2. Add all ingredients except basil leaves into the bowl and toss well.
3. Transfer vegetable mixture in parchment-lined baking pan.
4. Set to bake at 400 F for 35 minutes. After 5 minutes place the baking pan in the preheated oven.
5. Garnish with basil and serve.

Nutritional Value (Amount per Serving):

- Calories 96
- Fat 5.5 g
- Carbohydrates 11.7 g
- Sugar 6.4 g
- Protein 2.3 g
- Cholesterol 1 mg

Baked Cauliflower & Tomatoes

Preparation Time: 10 minutes

Cooking Time: 20 minutes

Serve: 4

Ingredients:

- 4 cups cauliflower florets
- 1 tbsp capers, drained
- 3 tbsp olive oil
- 1/2 cup cherry tomatoes, halved
- 2 tbsp fresh parsley, chopped
- 2 garlic cloves, sliced
- Pepper
- Salt

Directions:

1. Fit the Cuisinart oven with the rack in position 1.
2. In a bowl, toss together cherry tomatoes, cauliflower, oil, garlic, capers, pepper, and salt and spread in baking pan.
3. Set to bake at 450 F for 25 minutes. After 5 minutes place the baking pan in the preheated oven.
4. Garnish with parsley and serve.

Nutritional Value (Amount per Serving):

- Calories 123
- Fat 10.7 g
- Carbohydrates 6.9 g
- Sugar 3 g
- Protein 2.4 g
- Cholesterol 0 mg

Baked Apple Sweet Potatoes

Preparation Time: 10 minutes
Cooking Time: 30 minutes
Serve: 2

Ingredients:

- 2 large sweet potatoes, diced
- 2 tsp cinnamon
- 2 large green apples, diced
- 2 tbsp maple syrup
- 1 tbsp olive oil

Directions:

1. Fit the Cuisinart oven with the rack in position 1.
2. In a large bowl, add sweet potatoes, oil, cinnamon, and apples and toss well.
3. Spread sweet potatoes mixture in baking pan.
4. Set to bake at 400 F for 35 minutes. After 5 minutes place the baking pan in the preheated oven.
5. Drizzle with maple syrup and serve.

Nutritional Value (Amount per Serving):

- Calories 352
- Fat 7.6 g
- Carbohydrates 74 g
- Sugar 35.7 g
- Protein 2.2 g
- Cholesterol 0 mg

Jalapeno Bread

Preparation Time: 10 minutes

Cooking Time: 50 minutes

Serve: 10

Ingredients:
- 3 cups all-purpose flour
- 8 oz cheddar cheese, shredded
- 1/2 tsp ground white pepper
- 1 1/2 tbsp baking powder
- 1/4 cup butter, melted
- 1 1/2 cups buttermilk
- 3 jalapeno peppers, chopped
- 2 tbsp sugar
- 1 1/4 tsp salt

Directions:
1. Fit the Cuisinart oven with the rack in position 1.
2. In a mixing bowl, mix flour, baking powder, sugar, white pepper, and salt.
3. Add jalapenos and cheese and stir to combine.
4. Whisk butter and buttermilk together and add to the flour mixture. Stir until just combined.
5. Pour batter into the greased 9*5-inch loaf pan.
6. Set to bake at 375 F for 55 minutes. After 5 minutes place the loaf pan in the preheated oven.
7. Slice and serve.

Nutritional Value (Amount per Serving):
- Calories 297
- Fat 12.9 g
- Carbohydrates 34.5 g
- Sugar 4.5 g
- Protein 10.9 g
- Cholesterol 37 mg

Tasty Butternut Squash

Preparation Time: 10 minutes
Cooking Time: 15 minutes
Serve: 4

Ingredients:

- 4 cups butternut squash, cut into 1-inch pieces
- 1 tbsp brown sugar
- 2 tbsp olive oil
- 1 tsp Chinese 5 spice powder

Directions:

1. Fit the Cuisinart oven with the rack in position 2.
2. Toss squash into the bowl with remaining ingredients.
3. Transfer squash in the air fryer basket then places the air fryer basket in the baking pan.
4. Place a baking pan on the oven rack. Set to air fry at 400 F for 15 minutes.
5. Serve and enjoy.

Nutritional Value (Amount per Serving):

- Calories 132
- Fat 7.1 g
- Carbohydrates 18.6 g
- Sugar 5.3 g
- Protein 1.4 g
- Cholesterol 0 mg

Air Fried Eggplant Cubes

Preparation Time: 10 minutes
Cooking Time: 12 minutes
Serve: 2

Ingredients:
- 1 eggplant, cut into cubes
- 1/4 tsp oregano
- 1 tbsp olive oil
- 1/2 tsp garlic powder

Directions:
1. Fit the Cuisinart oven with the rack in position 2.
2. Add all ingredients into the large bowl and toss well.
3. Transfer eggplant into in air fryer basket then places the air fryer basket in the baking pan.
4. Place a baking pan on the oven rack. Set to air fry at 390 F for 12 minutes.
5. Serve and enjoy.

Nutritional Value (Amount per Serving):
- Calories 120
- Fat 7.4 g
- Carbohydrates 14.1 g
- Sugar 7.1 g
- Protein 2.4 g
- Cholesterol 0 mg

Cheese Herb Zucchini

Preparation Time: 10 minutes
Cooking Time: 15 minutes
Serve: 4

Ingredients:

- 4 zucchini, quartered
- 1/2 tsp dried oregano
- 2 tbsp fresh parsley, chopped
- 2 tbsp olive oil
- 1/2 tsp dried thyme
- 1/2 cup parmesan cheese, grated
- 1/4 tsp garlic powder
- 1/2 tsp dried basil
- Pepper
- Salt

Directions:

1. Fit the Cuisinart oven with the rack in position 1.
2. In a small bowl, mix parmesan cheese, garlic powder, basil, oregano, thyme, pepper, and salt.
3. Arrange zucchini in baking pan and drizzle with oil and sprinkle with parmesan cheese mixture.
4. Set to bake at 350 F for 20 minutes. After 5 minutes place the baking pan in the preheated oven.
5. Garnish with parsley and serve.

Nutritional Value (Amount per Serving):

- Calories 130
- Fat 9.8 g
- Carbohydrates 7.4 g
- Sugar 3.5 g
- Protein 6.1 g
- Cholesterol 8 mg

Parmesan Baked Asparagus

Preparation Time: 10 minutes

Cooking Time: 12 minutes

Serve: 4

Ingredients:

- 1 lb asparagus, wash, trimmed, and cut the ends
- 1 tbsp dried parsley
- 2 garlic cloves, minced
- 2 tbsp olive oil
- 3 oz parmesan cheese, shaved
- 1 tsp dried oregano
- Pepper
- Salt

Directions:

1. Fit the Cuisinart oven with the rack in position 1.
2. Arrange asparagus in baking pan. Drizzle with olive oil and season with pepper and salt.
3. Spread cheese, oregano, parsley, and garlic over the asparagus
4. Set to bake at 425 F for 17 minutes. After 5 minutes place the baking pan in the preheated oven.
5. Serve and enjoy.

Nutritional Value (Amount per Serving):

- Calories 155
- Fat 11.8 g
- Carbohydrates 6 g
- Sugar 2.2 g
- Protein 9.5 g
- Cholesterol 15 mg

Ranch Potatoes

Preparation Time: 10 minutes

Cooking Time: 20 minutes

Serve: 6

Ingredients:

- 1 1/2 lbs baby potatoes, cut in half
- 1/2 tsp paprika
- 1/2 tsp onion powder
- 1/2 tsp dill
- 1/2 tsp chives
- 1/2 tsp parsley
- 1/2 tsp garlic powder
- 2 tbsp olive oil
- 1/2 tsp salt

Directions:

1. Fit the Cuisinart oven with the rack in position 2.
2. Add baby potatoes and remaining ingredients into the mixing bowl and toss until well coated.
3. Transfer baby potatoes in air fryer basket then place air fryer basket in baking pan.
4. Place a baking pan on the oven rack. Set to air fry at 400 F for 20 minutes.
5. Serve and enjoy.

Nutritional Value (Amount per Serving):

- Calories 108
- Fat 4.8 g
- Carbohydrates 14.6 g
- Sugar 0.2 g
- Protein 3 g
- Cholesterol 0 mg

Baked Ratatouille

Preparation Time: 10 minutes

Cooking Time: 55 minutes

Serve: 6

Ingredients:

- 1 large eggplant, steamed and sliced
- 1/4 tsp dried thyme
- 2 bell pepper, sliced
- 4 tomatoes, sliced
- 2 tbsp olive oil
- 4 medium zucchini, sliced
- 1 tsp dried basil
- 1/2 tsp dried oregano

Directions:

1. Fit the Cuisinart oven with the rack in position 1.
2. Add all vegetable slices to a large bowl and season with salt and drizzle with oil.
3. Layer vegetable slices into the greased baking dish.
4. Set to bake at 400 F for 60 minutes. After 5 minutes place the baking dish in the preheated oven.
5. Sprinkle with dried herbs.
6. Serve and enjoy.

Nutritional Value (Amount per Serving):

- Calories 108
- Fat 5.3 g
- Carbohydrates 15.2 g
- Sugar 8.7 g
- Protein 3.5 g
- Cholesterol 0 mg

Chili Lime Sweet Potatoes

Preparation Time: 10 minutes

Cooking Time: 15 minutes

Serve: 4

Ingredients:

- 2 large sweet potatoes, peeled & cut into 1-inch pieces
- 1 tbsp chili powder
- 2 tbsp olive oil
- 2 tsp fresh lime juice
- 1 tsp cumin

Directions:

1. Fit the Cuisinart oven with the rack in position 2.
2. In a mixing bowl, add sweet potatoes, lime juice, cumin, chili powder, and olive oil and toss well.
3. Transfer sweet potatoes in air fryer basket then place air fryer basket in baking pan.
4. Place a baking pan on the oven rack. Set to air fry at 380 F for 20 minutes.
5. Serve and enjoy.

Nutritional Value (Amount per Serving):

- Calories 132
- Fat 1.1 g
- Carbohydrates 17.1 g
- Sugar 0.8 g
- Protein 1.2 g
- Cholesterol 0 mg

Broccoli Olives Tomatoes

Preparation Time: 10 minutes

Cooking Time: 10 minutes

Serve: 4

Ingredients:

- 4 cups broccoli florets
- 1/2 tsp lemon zest, grated
- 2 garlic cloves, minced
- 1 tbsp olive oil
- 1 tsp dried oregano
- 10 olives, pitted and sliced
- 1 tbsp fresh lemon juice
- 1 cup cherry tomatoes
- 1/4 tsp salt

Directions:

1. Fit the Cuisinart oven with the rack in position 1.
2. Add broccoli, garlic, oil, tomatoes, and salt in a large bowl and toss well.
3. Spread broccoli mixture onto the baking pan.
4. Set to bake at 450 F for 15 minutes. After 5 minutes place the baking pan in the preheated oven.
5. Meanwhile, mix together oregano, olives, lemon juice, and lemon zest in a mixing bowl.
6. Add roasted vegetables to the bowl and toss well.
7. Serve and enjoy.

Nutritional Value (Amount per Serving):

- Calories 86
- Fat 5.1 g
- Carbohydrates 9.4 g
- Sugar 2.9 g
- Protein 3.2 g
- Cholesterol 0 mg

Tasty Hassel Back Potatoes

Preparation Time: 10 minutes

Cooking Time: 30 minutes

Serve: 4

Ingredients:

- 4 potatoes, peel & cut potato across the potato to make 1/8-inch slices
- 1/4 cup parmesan cheese, shredded
- 1 tbsp olive oil

Directions:

1. Fit the Cuisinart oven with the rack in position 2.
2. Brush potatoes with olive oil.
3. Place potatoes in the air fryer basket then place an air fryer basket in the baking pan.
4. Place a baking pan on the oven rack. Set to air fry at 350 F for 30 minutes.
5. Sprinkle cheese on top of potatoes and serve.

Nutritional Value (Amount per Serving):

- Calories 195
- Fat 4.9 g
- Carbohydrates 33.7 g
- Sugar 2.5 g
- Protein 5.4 g
- Cholesterol 4 mg

Cheesy Squash Casserole

Preparation Time: 10 minutes

Cooking Time: 30 minutes

Serve: 6

Ingredients:

- 2 lbs yellow summer squash, cut into chunks
- 1/2 cup liquid egg substitute
- 3/4 cup cheddar cheese, shredded
- 1/4 cup mayonnaise
- 1/4 tsp salt

Directions:

1. Fit the Cuisinart oven with the rack in position 1.
2. Add squash in a saucepan then pour enough water in a saucepan to cover the squash. Bring to boil.
3. Turn heat to medium and cook for 10 minutes or until tender. Drain well.
4. In a large mixing bowl, combine together squash, egg substitute, mayonnaise, 1/2 cup cheese, and salt.
5. Transfer squash mixture into a greased baking dish.
6. Set to bake at 375 F for 35 minutes. After 5 minutes place the baking dish in the preheated oven.
7. Sprinkle remaining cheese on top.
8. Serve and enjoy.

Nutritional Value (Amount per Serving):

- Calories 130
- Fat 8.2 g
- Carbohydrates 7.7 g
- Sugar 3.5 g
- Protein 8 g
- Cholesterol 18 mg

Air-Fried Herb Mushrooms

Preparation Time: 10 minutes

Cooking Time: 25 minutes

Serve: 2

Ingredients:

- 1 lbs mushrooms, wash, dry, and cut into quarter
- 1 tbsp white vermouth
- 1 tsp herb de Provence
- 1/4 tsp garlic powder
- 1/2 tbsp olive oil

Directions:

1. Fit the Cuisinart oven with the rack in position 2.
2. Add all ingredients to the bowl and toss well.
3. Transfer mushrooms in the air fryer basket then place the air fryer basket in the baking pan.
4. Place a baking pan on the oven rack. Set to air fry at 350 F for 25 minutes.
5. Serve and enjoy.

Nutritional Value (Amount per Serving):

- Calories 99
- Fat 4.5 g
- Carbohydrates 8.1 g
- Sugar 4 g
- Protein 7.9 g
- Cholesterol 0 mg

Chapter 7: Snacks & Appetizers

Cheesy Spinach Dip

Preparation Time: 10 minutes
Cooking Time: 20 minutes
Serve: 12

Ingredients:

- 3 oz frozen spinach, defrosted & chopped
- 1 cup sour cream
- 1 tsp garlic salt
- 2 cups cheddar cheese, shredded
- 8 oz cream cheese

Directions:

1. Fit the Cuisinart oven with the rack in position 1.
2. Add all ingredients into the mixing bowl and mix well.
3. Transfer mixture into the baking dish.
4. Set to bake at 350 F for 25 minutes. After 5 minutes place the baking dish in the preheated oven.
5. Serve and enjoy.

Nutritional Value (Amount per Serving):

- Calories 185
- Fat 16.9 g
- Carbohydrates 2 g
- Sugar 0.3 g
- Protein 7 g
- Cholesterol 49 mg

Air Fryer Mixed Nuts

Preparation Time: 10 minutes

Cooking Time: 4 minutes

Serve: 2

Ingredients:

- 2 cup mixed nuts
- 1 tbsp olive oil
- 1 tsp ground cumin
- 1 tsp pepper
- 1/4 tsp cayenne
- 1 tsp salt

Directions:

1. Fit the Cuisinart oven with the rack in position 2.
2. In a bowl, add all ingredients and toss well.
3. Add the nuts mixture to the air fryer basket then place an air fryer basket in the baking pan.
4. Place a baking pan on the oven rack. Set to air fry at 350 F for 4 minutes.
5. Serve and enjoy.

Nutritional Value (Amount per Serving):

- Calories 953
- Fat 88.2 g
- Carbohydrates 33.3 g
- Sugar 6.4 g
- Protein 22.7 g
- Cholesterol 0 mg

Flavorful Crab Dip

Preparation Time: 10 minutes

Cooking Time: 15 minutes

Serve: 6

Ingredients:

- 6 oz crab lump meat
- 1 tbsp mayonnaise
- 1/8 tsp paprika
- 1/4 cup sour cream
- 4 tsp bell pepper, diced
- 1 tbsp butter, softened
- 1 tsp parsley, chopped
- 1 tbsp green onion, sliced
- 1/4 cup mozzarella cheese, shredded
- 4 tsp onion, chopped
- 2 oz cream cheese, softened
- 1/4 tsp salt

Directions:

1. Fit the Cuisinart oven with the rack in position 1.
2. In a bowl, mix together cream cheese, butter, sour cream, and mayonnaise until smooth.
3. Add remaining ingredients and stir well.
4. Pour mixture into the greased baking dish.
5. Set to bake at 350 F for 20 minutes. After 5 minutes place the baking dish in the preheated oven.
6. Serve and enjoy.

Nutritional Value (Amount per Serving):

- Calories 131
- Fat 10.8 g
- Carbohydrates 8.1 g
- Sugar 4.3 g
- Protein 6.4 g
- Cholesterol 37 mg

Jalapeno Spinach Dip

Preparation Time: 10 minutes

Cooking Time: 30 minutes

Serve: 6

Ingredients:

- 10 oz frozen spinach, thawed and drained
- 2 tsp jalapeno pepper, minced
- 1/2 cup cheddar cheese, shredded
- 8 oz cream cheese
- 1/2 cup onion, diced
- 2 tsp garlic, minced
- 1/2 cup mozzarella cheese, shredded
- 1/2 cup Monterey jack cheese, shredded
- 1/2 tsp salt

Directions:

1. Fit the Cuisinart oven with the rack in position 1.
2. Add all ingredients into the mixing bowl and mix until well combined.
3. Pour mixture into the 1-quart casserole dish.
4. Set to bake at 350 F for 35 minutes. After 5 minutes place the casserole dish in the preheated oven.
5. Serve and enjoy.

Nutritional Value (Amount per Serving):

- Calories 228
- Fat 19.8 g
- Carbohydrates 4.2 g
- Sugar 0.8 g
- Protein 9.7 g
- Cholesterol 61 mg

Vegetables Balls

Preparation Time: 10 minutes

Cooking Time: 10 minutes

Serve: 6

Ingredients:

- 2 cups cauliflower florets
- 1 tsp paprika
- 1 tsp chives
- 2 tsp garlic
- 1 medium Parsnip
- 1 medium carrot
- 1 cup breadcrumbs
- 1/2 cup desiccated coconut
- 2 tsp oregano
- 1 tsp mixed spice
- 1/2 cup sweet potato
- Pepper
- Salt

Directions:

1. Fit the Cuisinart oven with the rack in position 1.
2. Add all vegetables into the food processor and process until resemble breadcrumbs.
3. Add process vegetables into the mixing bowl.
4. Add all remaining ingredients into the bowl and mix well until combine.
5. Make small balls from the mixture and place in the air fryer basket then place an air fryer basket in the baking pan.
6. Place a baking pan on the oven rack. Set to air fry at 400 F for 10 minutes.
7. Serve and enjoy.

Nutritional Value (Amount per Serving):

- Calories 131
- Fat 2.7 g
- Carbohydrates 23.6 g
- Sugar 4.5 g
- Protein 4 g
- Cholesterol 0 mg

Zucchini Coconut Bites

Preparation Time: 10 minutes

Cooking Time: 10 minutes

Serve: 6

Ingredients:

- 4 zucchini, grated and squeeze out all liquid
- 1 cup shredded coconut
- 1 egg, lightly beaten
- 1 tsp Italian seasoning
- 1/2 cup parmesan cheese, grated

Directions:

1. Fit the Cuisinart oven with the rack in position 2.
2. Add all ingredients into the bowl and mix until well combined.
3. Make small balls from the zucchini mixture and place in the air fryer basket then place the air fryer basket in the baking pan.
4. Place a baking pan on the oven rack. Set to air fry at 400 F for 10 minutes.
5. Serve and enjoy.

Nutritional Value (Amount per Serving):

- Calories 105
- Fat 7.3 g
- Carbohydrates 6.8 g
- Sugar 3.2 g
- Protein 5.4 g
- Cholesterol 33 mg

Air Fryer Radish Chips

Preparation Time: 10 minutes

Cooking Time: 15 minutes

Serve: 12

Ingredients:

- 1 lb radish, wash and slice into chips
- 1/4 tsp pepper
- 2 tbsp olive oil
- 1 tsp salt

Directions:

1. Fit the Cuisinart oven with the rack in position 2.
2. Add all ingredients into the large bowl and toss well.
3. Add radish slices to the air fryer basket then place an air fryer basket in baking pan.
4. Place a baking pan on the oven rack. Set to air fry at 375 F for 15 minutes.
5. Serve and enjoy.

Nutritional Value (Amount per Serving):

- Calories 26
- Fat 2.4 g
- Carbohydrates 1.3 g
- Sugar 0.7 g
- Protein 0.3 g
- Cholesterol 0 mg

Crispy Eggplant Bites

Preparation Time: 10 minutes
Cooking Time: 20 minutes
Serve: 4

Ingredients:

- 1 eggplant, cut into 1-inch pieces
- 1 tsp garlic powder
- 2 tbsp olive oil
- 1/2 tsp Italian seasoning
- 1 tsp paprika
- 1/2 tsp red pepper

Directions:

1. Fit the Cuisinart oven with the rack in position 2.
2. Add all ingredients into the large mixing bowl and toss well.
3. Transfer eggplant mixture in air fryer basket then places air fryer basket in baking pan.
4. Place a baking pan on the oven rack. Set to air fry at 375 F for 20 minutes.
5. Serve and enjoy.

Nutritional Value (Amount per Serving):

- Calories 99
- Fat 7.5 g
- Carbohydrates 8.7 g
- Sugar 4.5 g
- Protein 1.5 g
- Cholesterol 0 mg

Healthy Baked Pecans

Preparation Time: 10 minutes

Cooking Time: 15 minutes

Serve: 8

Ingredients:

- 4 cups pecans
- 1/4 tsp onion powder
- 1/4 tsp garlic powder
- 4 tbsp fresh rosemary, chopped
- 1/4 cup olive oil
- 2 tsp lemon zest
- 1/4 tsp paprika
- 2 tsp Himalayan salt

Directions:

1. Fit the Cuisinart oven with the rack in position 1.
2. Add all ingredients except lemon zest into the large bowl and toss well.
3. Transfer pecans in baking pan.
4. Set to bake at 350 F for 20 minutes. After 5 minutes place the baking pan in the preheated oven.
5. Add lemon zest on top of roasted pecans and stir well.
6. Serve and enjoy.

Nutritional Value (Amount per Serving):

- Calories 269
- Fat 28 g
- Carbohydrates 5.6 g
- Sugar 1.2 g
- Protein 3.3 g
- Cholesterol 0 mg

Coconut Broccoli Pop-Corn

Preparation Time: 10 minutes

Cooking Time: 6 minutes

Serve: 4

Ingredients:

- 2 cups broccoli florets
- 4 eggs yolks
- 2 cups coconut flour
- 1/4 cup butter, melted
- Pepper
- Salt

Directions:

1. Fit the Cuisinart oven with the rack in position 2.
2. In a bowl whisk egg yolks with melted butter, pepper, and salt. Add coconut flour and stir to combine.
3. Coat each broccoli floret with egg mixture and place in the air fryer basket then place an air fryer basket in the baking pan.
4. Place a baking pan on the oven rack. Set to air fry at 400 F for 6 minutes.
5. Serve and enjoy.

Nutritional Value (Amount per Serving):

- Calories 201
- Fat 17.2 g
- Carbohydrates 7.7 g
- Sugar 1.4 g
- Protein 5.1 g
- Cholesterol 240 mg

Cheese Garlic Dip

Preparation Time: 10 minutes

Cooking Time: 20 minutes

Serve: 12

Ingredients:

- 4 garlic cloves, minced
- 5 oz Asiago cheese, shredded
- 1 cup sour cream
- 1 cup mozzarella cheese, shredded
- 8 oz cream cheese, softened

Directions:

1. Fit the Cuisinart oven with the rack in position 1.
2. Add all ingredients into the mixing bowl and mix until well combined.
3. Pour mixture into the baking dish.
4. Set to bake at 350 F for 25 minutes. After 5 minutes place the baking dish in the preheated oven.
5. Serve and enjoy.

Nutritional Value (Amount per Serving):

- Calories 157
- Fat 14.4 g
- Carbohydrates 1.7 g
- Sugar 0.1 g
- Protein 5.7 g
- Cholesterol 41 mg

Shrimp Kebabs

Preparation Time: 10 minutes

Cooking Time: 8 minutes

Serve: 2

Ingredients:

- 1 cup shrimp
- 1/4 tsp pepper
- 1/8 tsp salt
- 1 lime juice
- 1 garlic clove, minced

Directions:

1. Fit the Cuisinart oven with the rack in position 2.
2. Add shrimp and remaining ingredients into the bowl and toss well.
3. Thread shrimp onto the skewers and place in the air fryer basket then place an air fryer basket in the baking pan.
4. Place a baking pan on the oven rack. Set to air fry at 350 F for 8 minutes.
5. Serve and enjoy.

Nutritional Value (Amount per Serving):

- Calories 59
- Fat 0.8 g
- Carbohydrates 3.2 g
- Sugar 0.4 g
- Protein 9.9 g
- Cholesterol 90 mg

Air Fryer Nuts

Preparation Time: 10 minutes

Cooking Time: 9 minutes

Serve: 4

Ingredients:

- 1/2 cup macadamia nuts
- 1/4 cup walnuts
- 1/4 cup hazelnuts
- 1/2 cup pecans
- 1 tbsp olive oil
- 1 tsp salt

Directions:

1. Fit the Cuisinart oven with the rack in position 2.
2. Add all nuts to the air fryer basket then place an air fryer basket in the baking pan.
3. Place a baking pan on the oven rack. Set to air fry at 320 F for 9 minutes.
4. Drizzle nuts with olive oil and season with salt and toss well.
5. Serve and enjoy.

Nutritional Value (Amount per Serving):

- Calories 280
- Fat 29 g
- Carbohydrates 4.9 g
- Sugar 1.3 g
- Protein 4.7 g
- Cholesterol 0 mg

Air Fryer Paprika Almonds

Preparation Time: 5 minutes

Cooking Time: 6 minutes

Serve: 6

Ingredients:

- 1 cup almonds
- 1/4 tsp smoked paprika
- 2 tsp olive oil
- 1/4 tsp cumin
- 1 tsp chili powder

Directions:

1. Fit the Cuisinart oven with the rack in position 2.
2. Add almond into the bowl and remaining ingredients and toss to coat.
3. Transfer almonds in the air fryer basket then place an air fryer basket in the baking pan.
4. Place a baking pan on the oven rack. Set to air fry at 320 F for 6 minutes.
5. Serve and enjoy.

Nutritional Value (Amount per Serving):

- Calories 107
- Fat 9.6 g
- Carbohydrates 3.7 g
- Sugar 0.7 g
- Protein 3.4 g
- Cholesterol 0 mg

Cheddar Dill Mushrooms

Preparation Time: 10 minutes

Cooking Time: 5 minutes

Serve: 6

Ingredients:

- 9 oz mushrooms, cut stems
- 6 oz mozzarella cheese, shredded
- 1 tbsp butter
- 1 tsp dried parsley
- 1/2 tsp salt

Directions:

1. Fit the Cuisinart oven with the rack in position 2.
2. Add parsley, cheese, butter, and salt into the bowl and mix until well combined.
3. Stuff cheese mixture into the mushroom caps and place in the air fryer basket then place an air fryer basket in the baking pan.
4. Place a baking pan on the oven rack. Set to air fry at 400 F for 5 minutes.
5. Serve and enjoy.

Nutritional Value (Amount per Serving):

- Calories 141
- Fat 11.5 g
- Carbohydrates 1.9 g
- Sugar 0.9 g
- Protein 8.5 g
- Cholesterol 35 mg

Chapter 8: Desserts

Strawberry Cobbler

Preparation Time: 10 minutes
Cooking Time: 45 minutes
Serve: 6

Ingredients:

- 2 cups strawberries, diced
- 1 cup milk
- 1 cup self-rising flour
- 1 1/4 cup sugar
- 1 tsp vanilla
- 1/2 cup butter, melted

Directions:

1. Fit the Cuisinart oven with the rack in position 1.
2. In a bowl, mix together flour and 1 cup sugar.
3. Add milk and whisk until smooth.
4. Add vanilla and butter and mix well.
5. Pour mixture into the greased baking dish and sprinkle with strawberries and top with remaining sugar.
6. Set to bake at 350 F for 50 minutes. After 5 minutes place the baking dish in the preheated oven.
7. Serve and enjoy.

Nutritional Value (Amount per Serving):

- Calories 405
- Fat 16.5 g
- Carbohydrates 63.4 g
- Sugar 46 g
- Protein 4 g
- Cholesterol 44 mg

Delicious Raspberry Cobbler

Preparation Time: 10 minutes

Cooking Time: 10 minutes

Serve: 6

Ingredients:

- 1 egg, lightly beaten
- 1 cup raspberries, sliced
- 2 tsp swerve
- 1/2 tsp vanilla
- 1 tbsp butter, melted
- 1 cup almond flour

Directions:

1. Fit the Cuisinart oven with the rack in position 1.
2. Add raspberries into the baking dish.
3. Sprinkle sweetener over raspberries.
4. Mix together almond flour, vanilla, and butter in the bowl.
5. Add egg in almond flour mixture and stir well to combine.
6. Spread almond flour mixture over sliced raspberries.
7. Set to bake at 350 F for 15 minutes. After 5 minutes place the baking dish in the preheated oven.
8. Serve and enjoy.

Nutritional Value (Amount per Serving):

- Calories 66
- Fat 5 g
- Carbohydrates 3 g
- Sugar 1 g
- Protein 2 g
- Cholesterol 32 mg

Vanilla Butter Cake

Preparation Time: 10 minutes

Cooking Time: 30 minutes

Serve: 8

Ingredients:

- 1 egg, beaten
- 1/2 tsp vanilla
- 3/4 cup sugar
- 1 cup all-purpose flour
- 1/2 cup butter, softened

Directions:

1. Fit the Cuisinart oven with the rack in position 1.
2. In a mixing bowl, mix together sugar and butter.
3. Add egg, flour, and vanilla and mix until combined.
4. Pour batter into the greased baking dish.
5. Set to bake at 350 F for 35 minutes. After 5 minutes place the baking dish in the preheated oven.
6. Slice and serve.

Nutritional Value (Amount per Serving):

- Calories 211
- Fat 11 g
- Carbohydrates 27 g
- Sugar 16 g
- Protein 2 g
- Cholesterol 45 mg

Easy Blueberry Muffins

Preparation Time: 10 minutes

Cooking Time: 30 minutes

Serve: 12

Ingredients:

- 5.5 oz plain yogurt
- ½ cup fresh blueberries
- 2 tsp baking powder, gluten-free
- ¼ cup Swerve
- 2 ½ cups almond flour
- ½ tsp vanilla
- 3 eggs
- Pinch of salt

Directions:

1. Fit the Cuisinart oven with the rack in position 1.
2. Line 6-cups muffin tin with cupcake liners and set aside.
3. In a bowl, whisk egg, yogurt, vanilla, and salt until smooth.
4. Add flour, swerve and baking powder and blend again until smooth.
5. Add blueberries and stir well.
6. Pour batter into the prepared muffin tin.
7. Set to bake at 325 F for 35 minutes. After 5 minutes place muffin tin in the preheated oven.
8. Serve and enjoy.

Nutritional Value (Amount per Serving):

- Calories 63
- Fat 4.2 g
- Carbohydrates 3.6 g
- Sugar 1.8 g
- Protein 3.4 g
- Cholesterol 42 mg

Vanilla Banana Brownies

Preparation Time: 10 minutes
Cooking Time: 20 minutes
Serve: 12

Ingredients:

- 1 egg
- 1 cup all-purpose flour
- 4 oz white chocolate
- 1/4 cup butter
- 1 tsp vanilla extract
- 1/2 cup granulated sugar
- 2 medium bananas, mashed
- 1/4 tsp salt

Directions:

1. Fit the Cuisinart oven with the rack in position 1.
2. Add white chocolate and butter in a microwave-safe bowl and microwave for 30 seconds. Stir until melted.
3. Stir in sugar. Add mashed bananas, eggs, vanilla, and salt and mix until combined.
4. Add flour and mix until just combined.
5. Pour batter into the greased baking dish.
6. Set to bake at 350 F for 25 minutes. After 5 minutes place the baking dish in the preheated oven.
7. Slice and serve.

Nutritional Value (Amount per Serving):

- Calories 178
- Fat 7.4 g
- Carbohydrates 26.4 g
- Sugar 16.4 g
- Protein 2.3 g
- Cholesterol 26 mg

Mini Brownie Muffins

Preparation Time: 10 minutes
Cooking Time: 15 minutes
Serve: 6

Ingredients:

- 3 eggs
- 1/2 cup Swerve
- 1 cup almond flour
- 1 tbsp gelatin
- 1/3 cup butter, melted
- 1/3 cup cocoa powder

Directions:

1. Fit the Cuisinart oven with the rack in position 1.
2. Line 6-cups muffin tin with cupcake liners and set aside.
3. Add all ingredients into the mixing bowl and stir until well combined.
4. Pour mixture into the prepared muffin tin.
5. Set to bake at 350 F for 20 minutes. After 5 minutes place muffin tin in the preheated oven.
6. Serve and enjoy.

Nutritional Value (Amount per Serving):

- Calories 163
- Fat 15.4 g
- Carbohydrates 4 g
- Sugar 0.4 g
- Protein 5.8 g
- Cholesterol 109 mg

Cream Cheese Butter Cake

Preparation Time: 10 minutes
Cooking Time: 35 minutes
Serve: 8

Ingredients:

- 5 eggs
- 1 cup Swerve
- 4 oz cream cheese, softened
- 1 tsp vanilla
- 1 tsp orange extract
- 1 tsp baking powder
- 6.5 oz almond flour
- 1/2 cup butter, softened

Directions:

1. Fit the Cuisinart oven with the rack in position 1.
2. Add all ingredients into the mixing bowl and whisk until batter is fluffy.
3. Pour batter into the prepared cake pan.
4. Set to bake at 350 F for 40 minutes. After 5 minutes place the cake pan in the preheated oven.
5. Slices and serve.

Nutritional Value (Amount per Serving):

- Calories 325
- Fat 30.6 g
- Carbohydrates 6.2 g
- Sugar 1.2 g
- Protein 9.5 g
- Cholesterol 148 mg

Vanilla Lemon Cupcakes

Preparation Time: 10 minutes

Cooking Time: 15 minutes

Serve: 6

Ingredients:

- 1 egg
- 1/2 cup milk
- 2 tbsp canola oil
- 1/4 tsp baking soda
- 3/4 tsp baking powder
- 1 tsp lemon zest, grated
- 1/2 cup sugar
- 1 cup flour
- 1/2 tsp vanilla
- 1/2 tsp salt

Directions:

1. Fit the Cuisinart oven with the rack in position 1.
2. Line 12-cups muffin tin with cupcake liners and set aside.
3. In a bowl, whisk egg, vanilla, milk, oil, and sugar until creamy.
4. Add remaining ingredients and stir until just combined.
5. Pour batter into the prepared muffin tin.
6. Set to bake at 350 F for 20 minutes. After 5 minutes place muffin tin in the preheated oven.
7. Serve and enjoy.

Nutritional Value (Amount per Serving):

- Calories 200
- Fat 6 g
- Carbohydrates 35 g
- Sugar 17 g
- Protein 3 g
- Cholesterol 30 mg

Tasty Gingersnap Cookies

Preparation Time: 10 minutes

Cooking Time: 10 minutes

Serve: 8

Ingredients:

- 1 egg
- 1/2 tsp ground cinnamon
- 1/2 tsp ground ginger
- 1 tsp baking powder
- 3/4 cup erythritol
- 1/2 tsp vanilla
- 1/8 tsp ground cloves
- 1/4 tsp ground nutmeg
- 2/4 cup butter, melted
- 1 1/2 cups almond flour
- Pinch of salt

Directions:

1. Fit the Cuisinart oven with the rack in position 1.
2. In a mixing bowl, mix together all dry ingredients.
3. In another bowl, mix together all wet ingredients.
4. Add dry ingredients to the wet ingredients and mix until a dough-like mixture is formed.
5. Cover and place in the refrigerator for 30 minutes.
6. Make cookies from dough and place onto a parchment-lined baking pan.
7. Set to bake at 350 F for 15 minutes. After 5 minutes place the baking pan in the preheated oven.
8. Serve and enjoy.

Nutritional Value (Amount per Serving):

- Calories 142
- Fat 14.7 g
- Carbohydrates 1.8 g
- Sugar 0.3 g
- Protein 2 g
- Cholesterol 51 mg

Flavorful Coconut Cake

Preparation Time: 10 minutes

Cooking Time: 20 minutes

Serve: 8

Ingredients:

- 5 eggs, separated
- 1/2 cup erythritol
- 1/4 cup coconut milk
- 1/2 cup coconut flour
- 1/2 tsp baking powder
- 1/2 tsp vanilla
- 1/2 cup butter softened
- Pinch of salt

Directions:

1. Fit the Cuisinart oven with the rack in position 1.
2. Grease cake pan with butter and set aside.
3. In a bowl, beat sweetener and butter until combined.
4. Add egg yolks, coconut milk, and vanilla and mix well.
5. Add baking powder, coconut flour, and salt and stir well.
6. In another bowl, beat egg whites until stiff peak forms.
7. Gently fold egg whites into the cake mixture.
8. Pour batter in a prepared cake pan.
9. Set to bake at 400 F for 25 minutes. After 5 minutes place the cake pan in the preheated oven.
10. Slice and serve.

Nutritional Value (Amount per Serving):

- Calories 84
- Fat 5.9 g
- Carbohydrates 4.2 g
- Sugar 0.6 g
- Protein 4 g
- Cholesterol 102 mg

Orange Almond Muffins

Preparation Time: 10 minutes

Cooking Time: 20 minutes

Serve: 12

Ingredients:

- 4 eggs
- 1 tsp baking soda
- 1 orange zest
- 1 orange juice
- 1/2 cup butter, melted
- 3 cups almond flour

Directions:

1. Fit the Cuisinart oven with the rack in position 1.
2. Line 12-cups muffin tin with cupcake liners and set aside.
3. Add all ingredients into the large bowl and mix until well combined.
4. Pour mixture into the prepared muffin tin.
5. Set to bake at 350 F for 25 minutes. After 5 minutes place muffin tin in the preheated oven.
6. Serve and enjoy.

Nutritional Value (Amount per Serving):

- Calories 273
- Fat 24 g
- Carbohydrates 6 g
- Sugar 1 g
- Protein 2 g
- Cholesterol 75 mg

Almond Blueberry Bars

Preparation Time: 10 minutes

Cooking Time: 50 minutes

Serve: 4

Ingredients:

- 1/4 cup blueberries
- 3 tbsp coconut oil
- 2 tbsp coconut flour
- 1/2 cup almond flour
- 3 tbsp water
- 1 tbsp chia seeds
- 1 tsp vanilla
- 1 tsp fresh lemon juice
- 2 tbsp erythritol
- 1/4 cup almonds, sliced
- 1/4 cup coconut flakes

Directions:

1. Fit the Cuisinart oven with the rack in position 1.
2. Line baking dish with parchment paper and set aside.
3. In a small bowl, mix together water and chia seeds. Set aside.
4. In a bowl, combine together all ingredients. Add chia mixture and stir well.
5. Pour mixture into the prepared baking dish and spread evenly.
6. Set to bake at 300 F for 55 minutes. After 5 minutes place the baking dish in the preheated oven.
7. Slice and serve.

Nutritional Value (Amount per Serving):

- Calories 208
- Fat 18.2 g
- Carbohydrates 9.1 g
- Sugar 2.3 g
- Protein 3.6 g
- Cholesterol 0 mg

Strawberry Muffins

Preparation Time: 10 minutes

Cooking Time: 20 minutes

Serve: 12

Ingredients:

- 4 eggs
- 1/4 cup water
- 1/2 cup butter, melted
- 2 tsp baking powder
- 2 cups almond flour
- 2/3 cup strawberries, chopped
- 2 tsp vanilla
- 1/4 cup erythritol
- Pinch of salt

Directions:

1. Fit the Cuisinart oven with the rack in position 1.
2. Line 12-cups muffin tin with cupcake liners and set aside.
3. In a medium bowl, mix together almond flour, baking powder, and salt.
4. In a separate bowl, whisk eggs, sweetener, vanilla, water, and butter.
5. Add almond flour mixture into the egg mixture and mix until well combined.
6. Add strawberries and stir well.
7. Pour batter into the prepared muffin tin.
8. Set to bake at 350 F for 25 minutes. After 5 minutes place muffin tin in the preheated oven.
9. Serve and enjoy.

Nutritional Value (Amount per Serving):

- Calories 201
- Fat 18.5 g
- Carbohydrates 5.2 g
- Sugar 1.3 g
- Protein 6 g
- Cholesterol 75 mg

Easy Ricotta Cake

Preparation Time: 10 minutes

Cooking Time: 45 minutes

Serve: 8

Ingredients:

- 2 eggs
- 1/2 cup erythritol
- 1/4 cup coconut flour
- 15 oz ricotta
- Pinch of salt

Directions:

1. Fit the Cuisinart oven with the rack in position 1.
2. In a bowl whisk eggs.
3. Add remaining ingredients and mix until well combined.
4. Transfer batter in greased cake pan.
5. Set to bake at 350 F for 50 minutes. After 5 minutes place the cake pan in the preheated oven.
6. Slice and serve.

Nutritional Value (Amount per Serving):

- Calories 91
- Fat 5.4 g
- Carbohydrates 3.1 g
- Sugar 0.3 g
- Protein 7.5 g
- Cholesterol 57 mg

Tasty Pumpkin Cookies

Preparation Time: 10 minutes

Cooking Time: 25 minutes

Serve: 27

Ingredients:

- 1 egg
- 2 cups almond flour
- 1/2 tsp baking powder
- 1 tsp vanilla
- 1/2 cup butter
- 1 tsp liquid stevia
- 1/2 tsp pumpkin pie spice
- 1/2 cup pumpkin puree

Directions:

1. Fit the Cuisinart oven with the rack in position 1.
2. In a large bowl, add all ingredients and mix until well combined.
3. Make cookies from mixture and place onto a parchment-lined baking pan.
4. Set to bake at 300 F for 30 minutes. After 5 minutes place the baking dish in the preheated oven.
5. Serve and enjoy.

Nutritional Value (Amount per Serving):

- Calories 46
- Fat 4.6 g
- Carbohydrates 0.9 g
- Sugar 0.3 g
- Protein 0.7 g
- Cholesterol 15 mg

Conclusion

There's never been a simpler way to master the many features of the Cuisinart Convection Toaster Oven Air fryer. This Cuisinart Convection Toaster Oven Air fryer Cookbook is bursting with beginner basic guidance, hot tips, and tasty recipes and let this official guide show you how you can take your meals to the next level. There's never been a more convenient appliance than the Cuisinart Convection Toaster Oven Air fryer—or a better cookbook to pair with it.

Thank you for buying this Cuisinart Convection Toaster Oven Air fryer Cookbook. Now let's start your gourmet journey!

www.ingramcontent.com/pod-product-compliance
Lightning Source LLC
Chambersburg PA
CBHW081402070526
44583CB00020B/2641